An Infant Massage Guidebook

For Well, Premature, and Special Needs Babies

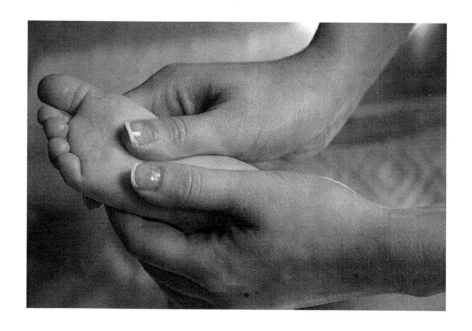

by

Mary Ady, CIMI

Certified Infant Massage Instructor (CIMI)

www.LittleLocalCelebrity.com

authorHOUSE®

AuthorHouse™
1663 Liberty Drive, Suite 200
Bloomington, IN 47403
www.authorhouse.com
Phone: 1-800-839-8640

First published by AuthorHouse 1/14/2008

ISBN: 978-1-4343-4060-3 (sc)

Library of Congress Control Number: 2007907841

Printed in the United States of America
Bloomington, Indiana

This book is printed on acid-free paper.

Note to the reader: This book is intended as an informational guide. The remedies,
approaches, techniques, and exercises described herein are meant to supplement, and not
to be a substitute for, professional medical care, treatment, or advice. They should not be
used to treat a serious ailment without prior consultation with a health care professional.

Photography: Courtesy of Charles W. Lytton, of National Geographic, Headshot by
Nathan Alger.

Design: Rafif Jouejati & Patrick Nolan of P3Solutions, and Jesse Williams, Graphic
Design Consultant.

For my mother and father, who taught me that
parenting is nothing if not selfless.

And for my daughter, Chloe Marie,
my heart, my soul, and our Lord Jesus Christ,
who showed me the purpose of my life.

Mary Ady with, the model of this book, her daughter Chloe
on Mother's Day 2007

Testimonials

"Repeat positive interactions between parent and child, such as those provided by infant massage, can result in positive physiological changes important for all mothers, especially those suffering from post-partum depression or anxiety."

— R. Nicolle Matthews, Ph.D. in Behavioral Neuroscience/ Psychology, Clinician of Behavioral Modification

"As a preschool teacher, I have spoken with numerous parents about infant massage. The parents truly feel infant massage helps to create and strengthen a life-long bond with their child. Parents that tried infant massage on their second child always seemed to mention the noticeable differences in the child's temperament and sleeping that lasted throughout their life. As a parent of twin daughters whom I practice infant massage with, I would have to agree!"

—Victorine Nicole Moon, BS in Child Adolescent Studies, Preschool Teacher at Beantree Learning in Ashburn, Virginia

"I can't even begin to tell you just how powerful the bond is that can be created between father and infant. My boys, A.J. (8 years) and Ethan, (5 years) received regular treatment from me (10 to 20 minutes a day) in the first nine months of life. I can tell you that in addition to the great bond that I have with them, they are very strong and emotionally healthy boys. I feel empowered as their father knowing that I made a significant contribution to their health that I would not otherwise be able to bring.

With mothers carrying so much of the brunt of early childhood development, there are not a lot of opportunities that we as fathers have to contribute. Today, my boys come to me for comfort as much, if not more, than they do from their mother. I feel that our bond is so much more than physical, it's emotional as well. The safety that they feel in my arms is truly incredible. I can't urge fathers enough to take advantage of this opportunity to give a gift that lasts a lifetime."

—John G. Louis, CMT, CIMI. (Mr. Louis is a certified massage therapist and certified infant massage instructor. He began his career with professional athletes in 1980. He founded Massage Therapy Center of Winnetka, Inc., and a highly regarded therapy clinic on the North Shore of Chicago, Illinois. He is also founder and CEO of Acuforce International, Inc., maker of innovative therapy equipment. He was the massage therapist for the 2005 World Series Champion Chicago White Sox Baseball team.)

"I hope everyone—planning, pregnant, or with an infant—reads this book. When a baby is born, touch is the primary means of communication, as it is fully developed by the time the baby as a fetus is 20 weeks old. Recent studies have proven that infant touch in the NICU not only promotes parental bonding but also shows benefits immediately—to include faster weight gain, increased body temperature stabilization, and improved oxygenation, which promotes earlier discharge by six days on average!"

—Cely Shields, RN

Acknowledgements

I personally wish to thank you for taking the time to learn more about Infant Massage. It will give you confidence when you have a routine your child acknowledges as one of comfort and love, such a skill that not only will help at all times with bonding but during trying times to relieve colic and over-tiredness. The fact that you are reading this book proves that you are one of the dedicated mothers in your community. I'm sure you have felt all the responsibility at times to raise your infant the best you can and the many different viewpoints, that change with every generation on how to best raise a child is ever-growing.

My mother told me every living thing needs love, you can't deny that. Infant Massage is a not about how to raise your child a certain way, it can be combined with any or without a plan- loving, educated touch will never be frowned upon. The great thing about Infant Massage is that it's considered a positive event for everyone. Infant Massage should be passed on as a family tradition, may it one day be referred to as an American tradition as much as it has been for centuries in India. Similar to warm milk, cuddling and bath time where there are some types of milk, cuddling and baths that you will find far better than others, Infant Massage can be ok or they can be extremely fun, build unity, make great moments of bonding and provide a superior service of love to the child.

The goal of Infant Massage has always been to provide a loving, comforting touch to your child and have fun doing it. If we take that one step further, to a higher level, we can create a daily event that everyone looks forward to and will generate a lifetime close-knit relationship.

If you follow the procedures in this book, your Infant Massage routine will run smoothly and effectively. These methods have helped countless families feel more bonded to their child. Follow these time tested methods and you will increase the level of parent-baby bonding you feel with your child and you will have everyone in your friend and family circuit hoping you will share your secret with them, when they see your child develop calmer and more relaxed through the months and years of their lives. You can count on that or my name isn't 'Chloe's Mommy.'

I wish to thank my mother Susan Marie (Woltman) Ady, and father Howard Parmele Ady, III. Through their dedication and support in making sure I finally finished this work and endless hours put in babysitting their granddaughter, it was all possible. Thanks to my parents for always being there, always with love and support. To Alison, Elizabeth, Miss Isabella Grace and Earle, I love you! Thanks to Laura Tomlinson, for everything and always being there.

Thanks to Charles Wayne Lytton who took the most amazing photos for my book, and Congratulations on his retirement from the National Geographic Society- You & Sue will be missed! My longtime friend Nathan Alger also did the author's photo and captured a good one. Thanks to Rafif Jouejati and Patrick Nolan at P3 Solutions and Jesse Williams for much needed Design and Graphic Consulting, as well as, Michelle Griggs who spent endless hours editing my work. Thanks to Nicolle Matthews, Vicki Moon, Cely Shields and John G. Louis who took time to read through and write me wonderful reviews. Thanks to the establishments who have let me hold my Infant Massage Workshops in the DC area, to include INOVA Alexandria Hospital where I gave birth to my daughter some six years after my first workshop there and for educating me over the years. Thanks to the American Massage Therapy Association (AMTA), the National Certification Board for Therapeutic Massage & Bodywork (NCTMB), Adam Eidlinger with Dr. Bronner's Magic Soap, for allowing me to participate at their booth during the DC Greenfestival 2006 with their wonderful team and organic products, and Tiffany Fields and her research team for information and understanding of the diversity of newborns within our industry. Thanks to the team of wonderful International Baccalaureate (IB) teachers at Mount Vernon High School, in particular my favorite teacher Bobbi Ingalls, George Mason University, Hardin-Simmons University, and the entire staff and students of the nationally acclaimed Potomac Massage Training Institute (PMTI) in Washington DC.

I would like to thank the Lord, Jesus Christ for endless grace and everything he has blessed me with, most importantly my daughter,

Chloe Marie Ady. Thanks to my church family at Calvary Road Baptist Church to include the entire Rhodenhizer family, in particularly Pastor Dave, Jason and Chris Rhodenhizer for sharing God's word and meaning with me. Thanks to the following people who have played very important roles in my life as a new believer in Christ: Debbie Arthur, Laura Doyle and the rest of my wonderful Tuesday night Bible Study Group: Tabitha, Greely, Bryan, Wendy, Atosha, Julia and Jessica. Christy Nielsen and the rest of the wonderful mothers at Image to include: Andrea, Rita, Dawn, Krista, Leslie, Shannon and Michelle. I would like to thank the many fabulous Women of the Word to include Debbie Arthur, Rebecca Lewis, Debbie Cox and a hundred others. I would also like to thank the entire Becker and Corvin families as a whole for being such a wonderful example of Joshua 24: 14-15, I will forever relate that verse to you all as a whole and hold you all dear to my heart. Thanks to Gina Miller for being the first growing-Christian I ever knew, and a wonderful babysitter!

"Before you were in the womb, I knew you; before you were born I set you apart." Jeremiah 1:5. Thanks to Peggy Jackson for providing a verse that brought me to my knees. A portion of the proceeds of this book will go to Calvary Road Baptist Church.

God Love, I do,

'Chloe's Mommy'

Mary Ady - Author. If you have innovative thoughts and unique perspectives, come think with Mary in the Online Blog and solve the Mommy and Daddy problems of the World; http://www.maryady.blogspot.com . Also, please check www.LittleLocalCelebrity.com often for current updates and resources for you and your baby!

Preface

This book is organized in 10 easy-to-read chapters complete with step-by-step photo illustrations to accompany the written infant massage instructions. This setup makes it simple to learn the infant massage routine—a routine that will enhance your relationship with your child. The book is accompanied with clear instructions on how to adapt the infant massage routine with specific techniques for use with preterm and special needs babies.

The book includes detailed references and a chapter dedicated to covering current research for the most common infant conditions in each of our eight body systems. This critical information is often missing from similar books on this subject. This book was written to help parents and caregivers learn the ancient technique of infant massage, and understand its broad range of benefits —not only for well babies, but for preterm babies and those with common health conditions, diseases, and disorders.

The routine includes specific techniques for common infant ailments such as colic. Please see the colic-relief routine in Chapter 5, which includes reflexology instruction for the feet, and Chapter 9, which covers Swedish massage strokes for the abdomen. Every reader can benefit from this book, whether you're a first-time parent or you're adopting your sixth child into your family. Topics include mastering your infant's non-verbal cues, aromatherapy for common infant ailments, and numerous helpful tips to comfort and soothe a colicky, high-needs infant.

The Resources section provides a list of many resources for pregnancy, post-partum, and parenting so that readers may further educate themselves and keep current on infant massage and infant wellness. I invite readers to access the latest scientific and education materials to supplement this book on my blog at www.maryady.blogspot.com. I will work to provide up-to-date information as you continue to add value to the quality of your child's life through infant massage.

I also invite you to share your thoughts, ideas, and comments on this book—as well as how your baby has responded to the infant massage routine taught in this book—on my website: www.LittleLocalCelebrity. com. You can also sign up for my newsletter and purchase my "Little Local Celebrity Organic (Jojoba) Massage Oil," and other items for you and your baby.

Contents

Chapter One: Introduction—History and General Benefits of Infant Massage for Infants and their Families

History of Infant Massage

Massage has been practiced since the dawn of mankind, and provides us with a tool to access our god-given, innate ability to soothe and comfort ourselves and others—literally in the palm of our hands. When you get a cramp in your foot, or any type of physical pain, you instantly and instinctively place your hands there and either hold it or rub the inflicted area to heal the pain. When you have emotional pain, you seek a hug, or a 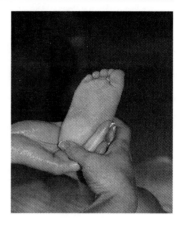 familiar hand to hold for a consoling, still touch to provide comfort.

In today's pharmaceutical world, it is sometimes hard for us to rely on a faith and trust in the healing powers that our own hands are capable of providing to those we love and hold dearest to us. Recently, it has been clinically proven through research (for non-believers in self-healing) that our hands have healing properties, when touch is applied with the intention to comfort and soothe and with a basic knowledge of effective techniques. The intensity of this desire to heal with touch can't be fully embraced until you hold a child in your arms who is in need of your care and loving touch. The foundation of infant massage has been around for centuries, innate in mankind, waiting for us to rediscover it.

"A young mother sat in the dirt with her baby across her knees, lovingly massaging him and singing. As I watched her I remember thinking, there is so much more to life than material wealth. She had so little, yet she could offer her baby this beautiful gift of love and security, a gift that would help to make him a compassionate human being.

I thought about all the children I had known there and how loving, warm, and playful they were in spite of their so-called disadvantages. They took care of each other and they accepted responsibility without reservation. Perhaps, I thought, they are able to be so loving, so relaxed and natural because they have been loved like this as infants, and infants have been loved like this in India for thousands of years.

A seed was planted in my mind, and I returned home with both joyful anticipation of the future and sadness for what I had to leave behind."

—from "A Short History of our Work" by Vimala McClure, founder of the International Association of Infant Massage

Within our society, in the span of less than a decade, we have seen a major transition in a woman's role in society. In our grandparents' era, which faded out slowly during our parents' era, a woman's role was strictly as a caregiver, as the main caretaker of husband, children, and home. Our grandmother's main desire was to stay home and teach her children manners, morals, religion, and character building. A home where she raised children she was proud of, in hopes that one day they would raise their own children with the same high expectations. Almost all women breastfed their infants and felt they were honored to have natural childbirth; the idea of being childless to save their bodies never crossed their minds.

These were very selfless, tenderhearted women who were proud to be mothers, who had learned these qualities from women as grand as they were, whom they affectionately called mother and grandmother.

Within two generations, that woman described above is lucky if she can find traces within herself of the woman she was raised to be. Over the span of just the last decade alone, that "instinctive" mothering trait, the result of what a society demands of woman, has drastically changed with an adverse impact on the parent-child relationship.

In today's society, the entire "working hours" are usually spent at work, leaving children to fend for themselves under another woman's care. Even stay-at-home mothers find themselves running from point A to point B, doing busywork and errands.... It is not surprising that most mothers feel they go through a whole day without some downtime to spend time individually bonding with their child.

Infant massage will provide you with a time for focused bonding with your child. It is time for mothers to free themselves from the demands of society, today, and to simply allow themselves to spend some quality time directly on their child through infant massage to begin the healthy lifelong relationship with their child they desperately need. The benefits far outweigh the cost, and you must make the time for this family investment for you and your child.

Infant massage is truly the key to establishing a nurturing, trusting, healthy relationship foundation with our children in the precious little time most parents are able to spend with their children in their earliest years, which will enable them to be a greater generation of mothers and fathers themselves.

Immediate and Life-long Benefits for Infants

My proven infant massage therapy routine will help your baby learn to relax by decreasing the production of stress hormones (lower cortisol and norepinephrine) and by increasing serotonin, the body's natural relaxation hormone, providing relaxation for your baby through the touch of your hands.[1] Your baby will soon establish the positive Pavlov conditioning pattern, creating a connection between your touch and their relaxation. After your first few massages with your child, she will become relaxed as soon as she recognizes that the massage is about to begin.

Besides the obvious relaxation response your baby will experience from the infant massage, your baby will also experience beneficial effects in each and every body system.

Infant massage will provide these additional full-body benefits:

- Infant massage promotes sounder and longer sleep patterns.[2]

- Infant massage helps improve sociability—a baby's disposition to enjoy the company of other babies their age. It helps comfort and soothe the infant, to set the stage for the development of a well-balanced, compassionate child, adolescent, and future adult.[3] Cross-cultural studies have shown many times over that infants who are held, massaged, carried, rocked, and breastfed grow up to be less aggressive and violent and more compassionate and cooperative. Preschool-age children with behavior problems who received massage are shown to have more focused on-task behavior, less solitary play, and less aggression.[4]

- Infant massage promotes habituation, or simple learning, by infants after only a few minutes of massage on the lower legs.[5] Habituation is what helps us learn to selectively attend to specific information and stimuli that are important, and to ignore that which is not. In one study, four-month-old infants were given either eight minutes of massage, play, or no stimulation prior to an audiovisual habituation task. Infants who received massage showed response recovery from habituation during test trials, whereas those in the other two conditions did not. The rate of habituation in babies is directly correlated with mental abilities in later development.[6]

As well as affecting every major body system, infant massage most importantly promotes parent-baby bonding and communication. Infant massage promotes eye contact between baby and parent. Infants showed more eye contact when adults who were smiling and cooing also massaged them, as compared to infants who received smiling and cooing without touch.[7]

Although all body systems are working in an interconnected manner to achieve and maintain a state of homeostasis (or balanced health) at all times, we will further categorize the benefits of infant massage by examining how each organ or body system is affected by infant massage in Chapter Two.

Benefits of Infant Massage for Parents and Grandparents

Infant massage promotes feelings of confidence in first-time parents as they realize they have the ability to help their child relax in times of stress or pain. This one-on-one time also helps parents begin to understand their child's non-verbal cues.

Infant massage promotes parent-baby bonding and communication by providing a time to focus on providing your baby with relaxation through touch. This is a great opportunity to promote father and baby bonding, as it will promote bonding for the baby and those who must be away for long periods of time during the day. In one study, fathers who gave their infants daily massages 15 minutes prior to bedtime for one month showed more optimal interaction behavior with their infants than those in the non-massage group.[28]

A common positive testimonial from a father who practiced infant massage with his children:

> "I can't even begin to tell you just how powerful the bond is that can be created between father and infant. My boys, A.J. (8 years) and Ethan, (5 years) received regular treatment from me (10 to 20 minutes a day) in the first nine months of life. I can tell you that in addition to the great bond that I have with them, they are very strong and emotionally healthy boys. I feel empowered as their father knowing that I made a significant contribution to their health that I would not otherwise be able to bring. With mothers carrying so much of the brunt of early childhood development, there are not a lot of opportunities that we as fathers have to contribute. Today, my boys come to me for comfort as much if not more than they do from their mother. I feel that our bond is so much more than physical, it's emotional as well. The safety that they feel in my arms is truly incredible. I can't urge fathers enough to take advantage of this opportunity to give a gift that lasts a lifetime."
>
> —John G. Louis, CMT, CIMI

Grandparents may even experience health benefits themselves after giving their grandson or granddaughter a massage. In a study, elderly retired volunteers were assessed after giving infants massage for a month versus receiving massage for a month themselves. They reported less anxiety, fewer depressive symptoms, and an improved mood after giving infants massage; their pulse decreased; their cortisol (stress hormone) levels decreased; and they reported improved self-esteem and a better lifestyle (e.g., fewer doctor visits and more social contacts) after the one-month period. These effects were stronger for those who gave infants massages than those who received massages themselves, suggesting that the massager can benefit from simply giving infant massages.[29] And of course a natural glow ensued, apparent to all those who know them, from falling into an unconditional, pure rapture of love with their new grandchild.

Chapter Two: Specific Health Benefits of Infant Massage for Infants with Common Health Conditions, Diseases, Disorders and Dysfunctional Body Systems

The Touch Research Institute, led by Tiffany Field, Ph.D., has conducted over 90 studies on the positive effects of massage therapy on many functions and how they relate to specific medical conditions and diseases. Among the most significant research findings on the benefits of infant massage are: enhanced growth in preterm infants, decreased autoimmune problems (a process where a child's immune system attacks the body's own tissues; for example, rheumatoid arthritis is an autoimmune disease), increased pulmonary (lung) function in asthma, and decreased glucose levels in infants and children with diabetes. Additional findings include: enhanced immune function, such as increased natural killer cells in HIV and cancer babies, enhanced alertness and performance in EEG pattern of alertness, and better performance on math computations. Many of these effects appear to be mediated by infant massage's clear ability to decrease stress hormones in the body.

Dr. Field's work has proven what we have always known—that educated hands have the power to heal.

You can access the institute's site at: http://www.miami.edu/touch-research/index.html. Donations are welcomed. Additional research references are available on their website concerning adolescents and adults as well as infants. For more information, contact: Touch Research Institute, University of Miami School of Medicine, P.O. Box 016820 Miami, FL 33101; phone: 305-243-6781; fax: 305-243-6488 ; e-mail: tfield@med.miami.edu.

The information listed below is provided as a resource and does not constitute an endorsement for any group. It is the responsibility of the reader, along with his or her child's pediatrician, to decide whether a group or resource is appropriate for each child's needs.

Circulatory (Cardiovascular) System

The main components of the circulatory system are the heart, the blood, and the blood vessels (arteries, capillaries and veins). The heart is a hollow, muscular pump that beats close to 60-100 times a minute or 100,000 times a day, more than 30 million times per year and about 2.5 billion times in a 70-year lifetime! The heart is responsible for propelling the circulation of blood throughout the body. The circulatory systems of all vertebrates (mammals which have a backbone or spinal cord, a skull, and an internal skeleton, such as humans) are closed, meaning that the blood never leaves the system of blood vessels.

We have two circulatory circuits: pulmonary circulation is a short loop from the heart to the lungs and back again, and the systemic system (the system we usually think of as our circulatory system) sends blood from the heart to all the other parts of our bodies and back again.

The blood is the "transportation system" for fuel, hormones, immune cells, nutrients, oxygen, and waste products from one part of the body to another. Blood is the fluid that carries the cells in circulation throughout the body. It passes from arteries to veins through capillaries, which are the thinnest and most numerous of the blood vessels. Arteries bring oxygenated blood to the tissues (except pulmonary arteries), and veins bring deoxygenated blood back to the heart (except pulmonary veins).

Each day 2,000 gallons (more than 7,570 liters) of blood travel many times through about 60,000 miles (96,560 kilometers) of blood vessels which branch out and cross, providing a link for all the cells of our organs and body parts to exchange. Blood includes cells that move from tissues to blood vessels and back, as well as to and from the spleen and bone marrow. Cells in the blood include red blood cells that carry oxygen, white blood cells that respond to infection and foreign substances, and platelets and plasma proteins that help blood clot and promote wound healing. There are also hormones produced in the circulatory system that help out other body systems. For example, one of the hormones produced by the heart helps control the kidney's release of salt from the body. The circulatory system also helps stabilize both the body's temperature and pH, which is an important part of homeostasis.

Common congenital heart defects (problems that are present at birth) found in infants and children:

> "Congenital heart defects, according to the March of Dimes, are the #1 occurring birth defect in the United States. Occurring in about 1 in every 115-150 live births; to put this in perspective, Down Syndrome occurs in about 1 in every 800-1,000 babies. Congenital heart defects are abnormalities in the heart's structure that are present at birth. For eight out of every 1,000 live births, there is a newborn born with a congenital heart defect. Congenital heart defects occur while the fetus is developing in the mother's uterus and although some cases are caused by genetic disorders, unfortunately it's still unknown why most of the cases occur. All congenital heart defects involve abnormal or incomplete development of the heart, ranging from as mild as a murmur that dissipates on its own, to needing a heart transplant."

> — *The Parent's Guide to Children's Congenital Heart Defects: What they are, how to treat them, how to cope with them* by Gerri Freid Kramer and Shari Maurer.

See also *Blue Lewis and Sasha, the Great* by Carol Donsky Newell.

Resource: CHD information and resources website: www.congenitalheartdefects.com

Common acquired heart defects (problems developed between infancy and adulthood; after birth) found in infants and children include:

- **Cardiomyopathy** is a chronic disease of the heart muscle that is caused by a genetic disorder or has an onset after an infection, in which the heart (the myocardium, the actual "heart muscle,") becomes weakened. The disease first affects the lower chambers of the heart, the ventricles, and then progresses and damages the muscle cells and even the tissues surrounding the heart, causing poor heart function. In its most severe forms, this condition may lead to heart failure and even death. Cardiomyopathy is the number one reason for heart transplants in children. Resource: Children's Cardiomyopathy Foundation—866-808-CURE; www.childrenscardiomyopathy.org

- **Kawasaki disease** affects the mucous membranes (the lining of the mouth and breathing passages), the skin, and the lymph nodes (part of the immune system) and may damage the heart muscle and coronary arteries. Kawasaki disease can also lead to vasculitis, which is an inflammation of the blood vessels. This can affect all major arteries in the body, including the coronary arteries, which supply blood to the heart. In the United States, Kawasaki disease has surpassed rheumatic fever as the leading cause of acquired heart disease in children. It is not contagious; the cause of Kawasaki disease is unknown but suspected to be caused by an abnormal reaction to a common germ. Resource: Kawasaki Disease Foundation, www.kdfoundation.org.

- **Myocarditis** is an inflammation of the myocardium, the thick muscular layer of the heart wall. When the coronary arteries become inflamed, a child can develop aneurysms, which are weakened and bulging spots on the walls of arteries. These increase the risk of a blood clot forming in the weakened area, which can block the artery, possibly leading to a heart attack. In addition to the coronary arteries, the heart muscle, lining, valves, or the outer membrane that surrounds the heart can become inflamed. Myocarditis is usually triggered by a viral infection such as the flu.

The American Heart Association, (www.americanheart.org 800-242-8721) is a great resource for educating your pre-kindergartner through eighth-grade child about the heart, with several fun songs and games. They also provide a link for parents to explore cardiovascular disorders, diseases, conditions, and treatments, as well as ideas on how to help your kids improve their lifestyle habits early on.

Making exercise part of your lifestyle, along with eating a nutritional diet, maintaining a healthy weight, and getting regular medical check-ups are the best ways to help keep the heart healthy and avoid many long-term lifelong cardiovascular struggles, including high blood pressure, high cholesterol, and heart disease. It is important that we as parents set an example for our children, taking preventative wellness measures in our lives as well.

Benefits of infant massage in the cardiovascular system:

- Enhances immune and filtering activities.

- Increases both your venous and lymphatic flow.

- Increases overall tissue fluid.

- Assists in lymphatic circulation to reduce swelling or contusions (bruises.)

- Facilitates tissue healing through increase in circulation.

- Increases the number of red blood cells in circulation, which causes an increase in hemoglobin and oxygen-carrying capacity of the blood.

- Lowers blood pressure and pulse.

- Increases the nutrition of the tissues through an exchange of fluids and materials.

- Produces dilation of blood vessels, which helps improve circulation.

- Direct pressure and stimulation through your touch reduces pain due to irritation of nerves that control your circulatory system.

- Increases your metabolism, thus enhancing the elimination of waste.

Endocrine System

The endocrine system consists of principal endocrine glands, including the pituitary, thyroid, adrenals, pancreas, parathyroids and gonads, as well as over 20 major hormones that are released directly into the bloodstream and that affect nearly every cell, organ, and function of the body.

The hypothalamus relays information sensed by the brain (such as environmental temperature, light exposure patterns, and feelings) to the pituitary, which acts as a "master hormone," because it makes hormones that control several other endocrine glands. It can also respond to emotional and seasonal changes. Among the hormones it releases are the human growth hormone, which stimulates growth of bone and tissue, and prolactin, which activates milk production in breastfeeding mothers.

The pituitary produces endorphins, chemicals that act on the nervous system to reduce sensitivity to pain. In addition, the pituitary secretes hormones that signal the ovaries and testes to make sex hormones. The pituitary gland also controls ovulation and the menstrual cycle in women, and it also produces oxytocin, which stimulates the contractions of the uterus in labor. The hormones of the thyroid control the rate at which cells burn fuels from food to produce energy. Thyroid hormones also play a key role in bone growth and the development of the brain and nervous system in children.

Parathyroids regulate the level of calcium in the blood. The adrenal glands have two different hormones: one that influences or regulates salt and water balance in the body, the body's response to stress, metabolism, the immune system, and sexual development and function; the second, adrenaline, increases blood pressure and heart rate when the body experiences stress.

The pineal body releases melatonin, which may influence the sleep-wake cycle. The gonads produce testosterone in males and estrogen and progesterone in women. The pancreas works to maintain a steady level of glucose, or sugar, in the blood and to keep the body supplied with fuel to produce and maintain stores of energy.

To summarize, the endocrine system is instrumental in regulating growth and development, tissue function, metabolism, and mood, as well as sexual function and reproductive processes. The endocrine system is in charge of body processes that happen slowly, such as cell growth, with faster processes like breathing and body movement monitored by the nervous system.

The right balance of hormones is key to maintaining homeostasis or balance within the body. For example, if the pituitary gland overproduces growth hormone, a child may grow excessively tall. If the pituitary gland underproduces growth hormone, a child may be abnormally short. Controlling the production of hormones, or replacing specific hormones, can treat many endocrine disorders and syndromes in children and adolescents.

Common endocrine disorders in infants and children include:

- Congenital adrenal hyperplasia is an adrenal insufficiency—a condition involving decreased function of the adrenal cortex and the resulting underproduction of adrenal corticosteroid hormone. About two-thirds of babies affected with congenital adrenal hyperplasia also do not produce enough of the salt-retention hormone, aldosterone, which can lead to dehydration, shock, and even death. Doctors treat adrenal insufficiency by giving replacement corticosteroid hormones to prevent these developments.

- Cushing syndrome occurs when excessive amounts of glucocorticoid hormones accumulate in the body. In children, it most often results when a child takes large doses of synthetic corticosteroid drugs (such as prednisone) to treat an autoimmune disease, such as lupus. It is referred to as Cushing's disease if the condition is due to a tumor in the pituitary gland that produces excessive amounts of corticotropin and stimulates the adrenals to overproduce corticosteroids. Symptoms may take years to develop and include obesity, growth failure, muscle fatigue, easy bruising of the skin, acne, high blood pressure, and psychological changes. Depending on the specific cause, doctors may treat this condition with surgery, radiation therapy, chemotherapy, or drugs that block the excessive production of hormones.

- Type 1 diabetes (previously known as juvenile diabetes) occurs when the pancreas fails to produce enough insulin. Symptoms include excessive thirst, hunger, urination, and weight loss. In children and teens, the condition is usually an autoimmune disorder in which specific immune system cells and antibodies produced by the child's immune system attack and destroy the cells of the pancreas that produce insulin. The disease can cause long-term complications including kidney problems, nerve damage, blindness, early coronary heart disease, and stroke. To control their blood sugar levels and reduce the risk of developing diabetes complications, children with this condition need regular insulin injections.

Infant massage benefits for infants and children with diabetes:

"Following one month of parents massaging their children with diabetes, the children's glucose levels decreased to the normal range and their dietary compliance increased. Also, the parents and children's anxiety and depression levels decreased.[21]"

Resources:

- Children with Diabetes Website, http://www.childrenwithdiabetes.com/ http://www.mychildhasdiabetes.com/

- American Diabetes Association: 1-800-DIABETES (1-800-342-2383). Hours of operation are Monday - Friday, 8:30 AM - 8 PM Eastern Standard Time. Or write to: American Diabetes Association, ATTN: National Call Center, 1701 North Beauregard Street, Alexandria, VA 22311. For diabetes-related questions or to request a diabetes information packet, email: AskADA@diabetes.org. In order to better serve you, please provide your name and address along with your request. www.diabetes.org.

- *My Child Has Diabetes: A Parent's Guide to a Normal Life After Diagnosis* by Karen Hargrave-Nykaza

- *Insulin-Dependent Diabetes in Children, Adolescents and Adults - How to become an expert on your own Diabetes* by Ragnar Hanas

> — *Even Little Kids Get Diabetes (An Albert Whitman Prairie Book)* by Connie Pirner and Nadine Westcott

> — *It's Time to Learn About Diabetes: A Workbook on Diabetes for Children*, Revised Edition by Jean Betschart-Roemer

- **Hyperthyroidism** is a condition in which there are extremely high levels of thyroid hormones in the blood. Symptoms may include weight loss, nervousness, tremors, excessive sweating, increased heart rate and blood pressure, protruding eyes, and a swelling in the neck from an enlarged thyroid gland. In children and teens, the condition is usually caused by Graves' disease, an autoimmune disorder in which specific antibodies produced by the child's immune system stimulate the thyroid gland to become overactive. Doctors may suggest treatment with medications or by removal or destruction of the thyroid gland through surgery or radiation treatments.

- **Primary congenital hypothyroidism** is a condition in which the levels of thyroid hormones in the blood are abnormally low. Thyroid hormone deficiency slows body processes so babies grow very slowly and may even have mental retardation. It may also lead to fatigue, a slow heart rate, dry skin, weight gain, constipation, and, in children, slowing of growth and delayed puberty. Hashimoto thyroiditis, which results from an autoimmune process that damages the thyroid and blocks thyroid hormone production, is the most common cause of hypothyroidism in children. Infants can also be born with an absent or underdeveloped thyroid gland, resulting in hypothyroidism. The condition can be treated with oral thyroid hormone replacement. Resource: The Endocrine Society, www.endo-society.org; 301-941-0200.

Gastrointestinal and Urinary Systems

The gastrointestinal system consists of the mouth, esophagus, stomach, intestines (small and large), the rectum, liver, pancreas, gallbladder, and salivary glands. The purpose of the gastrointestinal system is to convert food into small, nutritional molecules for distribution via circulation to all of the tissues of the body and to excrete unused residue as waste.

The urinary system consists of the bladder, kidneys, ureters, and urethra. The urinary system removes water from the blood to produce urine, which carries a variety of waste molecules and excess ions (such as calcium, sodium, and potassium) and water out of the body.

Everyone has a digestive problem at one time or another; indigestion, constipation, and mild diarrhea are common. Common digestive problems result in mild discomfort and get better on their own or are easy to treat. Others, such as inflammatory bowel disease, can be long-lasting or troublesome, in which case you may need to see a doctor who specializes in the digestive system, such as a GI specialist or gastroenterologist.

Some common disorders of the gastrointestinal system found in infants and children:

- **Celiac** disease is an autoimmune disease, in which a person's digestive system is damaged by the response of the immune system to a protein called gluten, which is found in barley, rye, and oats, that damages the lining of the digestive system and interferes with nutrient absorption. Babies with celiac disease have difficulty digesting the nutrients from their milk/formula and/or food and may experience abdominal pains, loss of appetite, severe diarrhea, malnutrition, irritability, failure to grow or gain weight and/or a skin rash. In more severe cases, failure to thrive and anorexia may also be present. The symptoms can be managed by following a strict, lifelong gluten-free diet, which is essential to reduce the chance of developing gastrointestinal malignancies. Celiac disease is genetic and can become active after some sort of stress, such as surgery or a viral infection. A doctor can diagnose celiac disease with a blood test and by taking a complete medical history; it is often correlated with diabetes and other autoimmune diseases.

<u>Resources:</u>

- <u>Clan Thompson's Celiac Site (www.clanthompson.com, link has gluten-free food and drug lists, recipes, FAQ's, information for celiac vegetarians, and lots of other valuable information.</u>

— Gluten Free Works Store has over 200 Gluten-free/ Cane Sugar free foods that are natural or organic: www. glutenfreeworks.com.

- **Colic:** Although the reason for its occurrence is still unclear, the theory most agreed on by experts is that colic is the result of an oversensitivity to gas in the intestine that occurs when an infant is crying for a sustained period of time due to trouble transitioning from one sleep state to another. Colic is defined in a baby less than three months old that has a period of inconsolable crying lasting hours at a time for at least three weeks. If your baby seems to be passing more gas it may be that she may be swallowing too much air when crying or feeding. Other theories for colic include milk allergy and temperament with adjusting to their new environment.

If your baby has colic, try the colic-relief routine provided in this book for relief of gas. If your baby has colic, be sure to have a friend or family member come over so you can have a break during the day. You can try Colic-ease Gripe Water or Mylicon, but please consult with your child's pediatrician first. Resource: Online Colic Support Group (www.colicsupport.com) has free help from other parents, including colic product review and useful websites.

- **Gastroesophageal reflux disease** (GERD), commonly referred to as "reflux," is a condition in which the esophageal sphincter (the tube of muscle that connects the esophagus with the stomach) allows the acidic contents of the stomach to move backward up into the esophagus, which becomes raw and irritated through this process. GERD can sometimes be corrected through lifestyle changes, such as adjusting the types of things a person eats. Things that may help a baby with reflux include feeding smaller amounts more often, feeding slowly with baby upright, raising the head of the bed, and handling your baby gently after a feeding. Sometimes it may require treatment with medication. Resource: The Pediatric/ Adolescent Gastroesophageal Reflux Association (www.reflux.org) is a great source of information. The site provides a Kid's Room with a GERD book online, Information on Going to School with Acid Reflux, Coping with GERD and more.

- **Hepatitis** is a viral condition in which a person's liver can become inflamed, have scarring, cirrhosis, cancer, and even lose its overall ability to function.

<u>Resources</u>:

- Hepatitis Neighborhood (www.hepatitisneighborhood.com) has a pediatric hepatitis link with a lot of helpful information.

- Hepatitis B Foundation (www.hepb.org (215) 489-4900)

- **Irritable bowel syndrome (IBS)** is a gastrointestinal disorder that affects a child's colon and may cause recurrent discomfort and abdominal cramps, bloating, constipation, diarrhea, and overall altered bowel habits. There is no cure for IBS, but the symptoms may be treated by changing eating habits, reducing stress, and making lifestyle changes. Resource: The American Urological Association, Pediatric Conditions page (www.urologyhealth.org/pediatric/) has information on urologic diseases and conditions.

The kinds and amounts of food a person eats and how the digestive system processes that food play key roles in maintaining good health. Eating a healthy, nutritious diet is the best way to prevent common digestive problems.

Benefits of infant massage on the gastrointestinal and urinary systems:

- Incorporates specific techniques tailored to relieve discomfort from colic and gas pains in the abdomen and its underlying intestinal tract.

- Facilitates elimination through large intestines by mechanically stimulating peristalsis propelling food from the esophagus thru the intestines.

- Improves gastrointestinal tract tone, reduces cramping and spasm.

- It increases the excretion in the kidneys of fluids and waste products of protein metabolism: urea (from protein catabolism) and uric acid (from nucleic acid metabolism).

Immune System

The immune system consists of the white blood cells, the thymus, lymph nodes, and lymph channels, which are also part of the lymphatic system. The immune system provides a mechanism for the body to distinguish its own cells and tissues from alien cells and substances and to neutralize or destroy the latter by using specialized proteins such as antibodies, cytokines, and receptors, among many others.

Disorders of the immune system can be broken down into four main categories: immunodeficiency disorders (primary or acquired), autoimmune disorders (in which the body's own immune system attacks its own tissue as foreign matter), Allergic disorders (in which the immune system overreacts in response to an antigen), and cancers of the immune system.[1]

Immunodeficiencies occur when a part of the immune system is not present or is not working properly. Sometimes a person is born with an immunodeficiency—these are called primary immunodeficiencies. Although primary immunodeficiencies are conditions that a person is born with, symptoms of the disorder sometimes may not show up until later in life. Immunodeficiencies can also be acquired through infection or produced by drugs. These are sometimes called secondary or acquired immunodeficiencies.

Some examples of primary immunodeficiencies that can affect babies, kids, and teens are:

- **Immunogloubin A (IgA) deficiency** is the most common type of primary immunodeficiency disorder. IgA is an immunoglobulin that is found primarily in the saliva and other body fluids that help guard the entrances to the body. IgA deficiency is a disorder in which the body doesn't produce enough of the antibody IgA. People with IgA deficiency tend to have allergies or get more colds and other respiratory infections due to their lowered immune system, but the condition is usually not severe or life-threatening, but may require monthly IV immunoglobulin (antibody) injections or infusions and prophylactic antibiotics.

- **Severe combined immunodeficiency (SCID)** is also known as the "bubble boy" disease (after a Texas boy with SCID who lived in a germ-free plastic bubble). SCID occurs due to a lack of both B and T lymphocytes, which makes it almost impossible to fight infections. Treatment consists of bone marrow transplants, avoiding live viral vaccines, and possible treatment with monthly immunoglobulin (antibody) injections.

Acquired immunodeficiencies usually develop after a person has a disease, although they can also be the result of malnutrition, burns, or other medical problems. Certain medicines also can cause problems with the functioning of the immune system. Some examples of secondary immunodeficiencies are:

- **HIV (human immunodeficiency virus) infection/AIDS (acquired immunodeficiency syndrome)** is a disease that slowly and steadily destroys the immune system. It is caused by HIV, a virus which wipes out certain types of lymphocytes called T-helper cells. Without T-helper cells, the immune system is unable to defend the body against normally harmless organisms. This loss of defense cells can cause life-threatening infections in people who have HIV. Newborns can get HIV infection from their mothers while in the uterus, during the birth process, or during breastfeeding. Every year, more than 700,000 children become HIV-positive via transmission from their parents. For the newborns exposed, increased weight gain and improved performance on the Brazelton Newborn Scale (motor and state scales) were experienced by the massaged newborns.[23] Natural killer cells (CD4 cells and CD4/CD8 ratio) increased after one month of massage therapy for adolescents with HIV, suggesting positive effects on the immune system.

Resources:

- http://www.womenchildrenhiv.org/

- 24-Hour National HIV/AIDS Hotline: 800-342-AIDS (800-342-2437) For calls outside the U.S.: 301-217-0023

- 24-Hour Spanish HIV/AIDS Hotline: 800-344-SIDA (800-344-7432)

- For more resources on HIV and the family please contact Women and Family Services Department at GMHC: 212-367-1366. To reach Just Kids Foundation please call 914-934-9254 or 718-892-4634.

- *Built To Survive: HIV Wellness Guide, Fourth Edition* by Michael Mooney and Nelson Vergel

- *The First Year--HIV: An Essential Guide for the Newly Diagnosed* by Brett Grodeck and Daniel S. Berger

Immunodeficiencies can be caused by medications. There are several medicines that suppress the immune system. One of the drawbacks of chemotherapy treatment for cancer, for example, is that it not only attacks cancer cells, but other fast-growing, healthy cells, including those found in the bone marrow and other parts of the immune system. In addition, people with autoimmune disorders or who have had organ transplants may need to take immunosuppressant medications. These medicines can also reduce the immune system's ability to fight infections and can cause secondary problems.

In autoimmune disorders, the immune system mistakenly attacks the body's healthy organs and tissues as though they were foreign invaders. Some examples of autoimmune diseases:

- Juvenile rheumatoid arthritis is a disease in which the child's immune system acts as though certain body parts such as the joints of the knee, hand, and foot are foreign tissue and attacks them. Resource: www.raliving.com.

- **Lupus** is a chronic autoimmune disease marked by flare-ups of muscle and joint pain and inflammation. The abnormal immune response may also involve attacks on the kidneys and other organs. Resource: Systemic Lupus Erythematosus in Pediatrics Website (www.kidlupus.org)

- **Multiple Sclerosis (MS)**—symptoms of MS are unpredictable and vary from person to person and from time to time in the same person. For example, one person may experience abnormal fatigue, while another might have severe vision problems. A person with MS could have loss of balance and muscle coordination making walking difficult; another person with MS could have slurred speech, tremors, stiffness, and bladder problems. While some symptoms will come and go over the course of the disease, others may be more lasting. In children with multiple sclerosis, massage therapy decreased anxiety and depressed mood, improved self-esteem, body image and social functioning.[25]

Resources:

- Children's Hope for Understanding Multiple Sclerosis. CHUMS http://www.chumsweb.org/

- National MS Society, http://www.nationalmssociety.org 1-800 FIGHT MS

- *Multiple Sclerosis Q & A: Researching Answers to FAQs* by Beth Ann Hill

- *The First Year-Multiple Sclerosis: An Essential Guide for the Newly Diagnosed (The First Year Series)* by Margaret Blackstone

- *Multiple Sclerosis: Everything You Need To Know (Your Personal Health)* by Paul O'Connor

Allergic disorders occur when the immune system overreacts to exposure to antigens in the external environment. The substances that provoke such attacks are called allergens. The immune response can cause symptoms such as swelling, watery eyes, and sneezing, and even a life-threatening reaction called anaphylaxis. Taking medications called antihistamines can relieve most symptoms.

Example of a common allergic disorder: Eczema is a scaly, itchy rash also known as Atopic Dermatitis. Although Atopic Dermatitis is not necessarily caused by an allergic reaction, it more often occurs in kids and teens who have allergies, hay fever, or asthma or who have a family history of these conditions.

Cancer occurs when cells grow out of control. This can also happen with the cells of the immune system. Lymphoma involves the lymphoid tissues and is one of the more common childhood cancers. Leukemia, which involves abnormal overgrowth of leukocytes, is the most common childhood cancer. With current medications most cases of both types of cancer in kids and teens are curable.

Benefits of infant massage on infants and children with leukemia:

- Twenty children with leukemia were provided with daily massages by their parents and were compared to a standard treatment control group. Following a month of massage therapy, distress during medical procedures decreased, depressed mood decreased in the children's parents, and the children's white blood cell and neutrophil counts increased.[24]

Resources:

- Saint Jude Children's Research Hospital, http://www. stjude.org/leukemia 1-866-2ST-JUDE (1-866-278-5833)

- American Cancer Society 800-227-2345.

- Association of Cancer Online Resources (ACOR) http:// leukemia.acor.org has Internet Support Email Lists.

- National Cancer Institute, www.cancer.gov is an informational website from the NIH.

- *Surviving Leukemia: A Practical Guide (Your Personal Health)* by Robert Patenaude

— *Having Leukemia Isn't So Bad: Of Course It Wouldn't Be My First Choice* by Cynthia Krumme

The decreased cortisol (stress hormone) level associated with infant massage may be attributed to improved immune function, as cortisol destroys immune cells.

Although immune system disorders usually can't be prevented, you can help your child's immune system stay strong and fight illnesses by staying informed about your child's condition and working closely with your child's doctor.

Integumentary System (Skin)

The skin is the largest organ of the body, accounting for somewhere between 12 and 15 percent of your entire body weight. The skin is responsible for guarding all underlying muscles and organs. The average square inch of skin holds 650 sweat glands, 20 blood vessels, 60,000 melanocytes, and more than a thousand nerve endings. The skin is our first line of defense. It serves as an interface with our external environment, protecting us against many pathogens in our everyday life such as chemicals, dirt, germs and pollution; Langerhans cells in the skin are part of the adaptive immune system.

The skin also functions in temperature regulation; the skin contains an immense blood reservoir that allows precise control of heat regulation to minimize energy loss by radiation, convection, and conduction. Blood vessels play an important role in this aspect. When the blood vessels dilate, perfusion is increased and heat loss results; when the blood vessels are constricted, the cutaneous blood flow is reduced which conserves heat. Arrector pilli muscles contract and cause us to shiver, which generates heat and causes our hair to stand up as "goose bumps."

Sweating is the process that allows the skin to excrete the waste urea in a concentration of about 1/130th that of urine. The skin also absorbs oxygen, nitrogen, and carbon dioxide in small amounts by diffusion. The skin can store water and also provides an impermeable barrier to fluid evaporation, which is why skin that is burned suffers massive fluid loss. Besides water, the skin can store lipids and synthesize vitamins D and B through exposure to the sun's UV rays on certain parts of the skin; this vitamin synthesis is what produces pigmentation (color), with lighter skin producing more D than B and vice versa.

Because the skin is an impermeable barrier which can absorb, medications can be administered through the skin, through ointments, or by means of an adhesive patch. The skin contains a wide variety of nerve endings for sensation, reacting to heat and tissue injury as well as touch, pressure, and vibration. The skin is also important in communications as a means for others to observe our mood and physical state as well as attractiveness.

Some common conditions children can get when things go wrong with the skin, hair and nails:

- Dermatitis—medical experts use the term dermatitis to refer to any inflammation (swelling, itching, and redness) of the skin. There are many types of dermatitis, including:

   - Eczema is a common, hereditary dermatitis that causes an itchy rash on various parts of the body. It commonly develops in infancy, but can also appear in early childhood. It may be associated with allergic diseases, such as asthma.

   - Seborrheic dermatitis is an oily rash on the scalp, face, chest, and groin area, caused by an overproduction of sebum from the sebaceous glands. This condition is common in young infants and adolescents.

Benefits of infant massage on disorders of the skin:

- "After receiving massage, children's affect (emotional state) and activity levels improved, as did all measures of skin condition to include: less redness, lichenification (thickened skin that is produced by excessive scratching), excoriation (a hollowed out or linear scab caused by scratching), and pruritis (itching.) Parents' anxiety levels also decreased.[20]"

25

> — <u>*Under my skin: A kid's guide to atopic dermatitis* by Karen Crowe</u>
>
> <u>Resource: 21st Century Complete Medical Guide to Eczema, Atopic Dermatitis, Authoritative Government Documents, Clinical References, and Practical Information for Patients and Physicians (CD-ROM), by PM Medical Health News</u>

Fungal infections of the skin and nails:

- **Candidal dermatitis** occurs in a warm, moist environment, such as that found in the folds of the skin in the diaper area of infants, providing a perfect environment to promote the growth of the yeast *Candida.*

Other skin problems include:

- **Acne** (acne vulgaris) is the single most common skin condition in teens. Some degree of acne is seen in 85 percent of adolescents, and nearly all teens have the occasional pimple, blackhead, whitehead or blemish.

- **Parasitic infestations** (usually tiny insect or worm parasites) can feed on or burrow into the skin, often resulting in an itchy rash. Scabies and lice are examples of parasitic infestations. Both are contagious - meaning they can be easily caught and transferred to and from other people.

- **Viral infections:** Many viruses cause characteristic rashes on the skin. Examples include: Varicella, the virus that causes chickenpox and shingles; Herpes simplex, which causes cold sores; Papillomavirus, the virus that causes warts; among others.

In addition to these diseases and conditions, the skin can be injured in a number of ways. Minor scrapes, cuts, and bruises heal quickly on their own, but other injuries—severe cuts and burns, for example—require medical treatment.

Benefits of infant massage to burn victims:

- When children suffer burns, massage therapy given prior to dressing young children's (mean age = 2.5 years old) severe body burns decreased distress behaviors. Nurses also reported greater ease from beginning to end of the dressing change procedure for the children in the massage group. The massage was conducted to body parts that were not affected with burns.[15] Post burn Symptoms: Massage therapy given to burn patients reduced anxiety, itching, pain, and improved mood immediately after the very first and last therapy sessions, and their ratings on each of these measures improved steadily from the first day to the last day of the study.[16]

Resources:

- Burned Children Recovery Foundation at http://www. burnchildrenrecovery.org/ 1.800.799.BURN

- Surviving Burns Support Services, Inc. (SBSS) is a burn survivor support group outreach for mentoring burn survivors of all ages, and their friends and family: http:// www.survivingburns.org/ (520) 886-4693

Disorders of the scalp and hair:

- **Alopecia** is an area of hair loss. Ringworm is a common cause of temporary alopecia in children. Alopecia can also be caused by tight braiding that pulls on the hair roots (this condition is called tension alopecia). Alopecia areata (where a person's hair falls out in round or oval patches on the scalp) is a rarer condition that can affect children and teens.

- **Tinea capitis,** a type of ringworm, is a fungal infection that forms a scaly, ring-like lesion in the scalp. It's contagious and common among school-age children.

Benefits of infant massage to the integumentary system:

- Infant massage helps to reduce tension build-up and stress in the skin and all underlying tissues.

- Increases circulation through the layers, as well as improved overall nutrition.

- Helps to re-moisturize and soften dry skin with natural oils and helps with some skin conditions such as eczema, which can be amplified by application of specific oils such as bergamot, lavender and evening primrose essential oils.

Nervous System

The nervous system consists of the central nervous system (CNS,) which is the brain and spinal cord, and the peripheral nervous system (PNS,) which contains only nerves and connects the brain and spinal cord (CNS) to the rest of the body.

The brain is the organ of emotion, thought, and sensory processing, and serves many aspects of communication and control of various other systems and functions. Because the brain controls just about everything, when something goes wrong with it, it's often serious and can affect many different parts of the body. Genetic diseases, brain disorders associated with mental illness, and head injuries can all affect the way the brain works and upset the daily activities of the rest of the body.

Common problems that can affect the brain and nervous system in infants and children include:

- **Cerebral palsy** is the result of a developmental defect or damage to the brain before or during birth. It affects the motor areas of the brain. A person with cerebral palsy may have average intelligence or can have severe developmental delays or mental retardation. Cerebral palsy can affect body movement in many different ways. In mild cases of cerebral palsy, there may be minor muscle weakness of the arms and legs. In other cases, there may be more severe motor impairment - a child may have trouble talking and performing basic movements like walking. Massage therapy helped children with cerebral palsy reduce spasticity (involuntary muscle tightness and stiffness that occurs in about two-thirds of people with cerebral palsy generally in the lower limbs), gain more muscle flexibility and motor function. They also have more positive social interaction.[17] Your child's occupational or physical therapist can go over which of the infant massage techniques are best for your child.

Resources:

- United Cerebral Palsy, http://www.ucp.org/

- American Academy for Cerebral Palsy and Developmental Medicine (AACPDM), http://www.aacpdm.org/

- *Cerebral Palsy: A Complete Guide for Caregiving* (A Johns Hopkins Press Health Book) by Freeman Miller and Steven J. Bachrach

- *My Perfect Son Has Cerebral Palsy: A Mother's Guide of Helpful Hints* by Marie Kennedy

- *Children With Cerebral Palsy: A Parents' Guide* by Elaine Geralis

- **Epilepsy or seizure disorder** is made up of a wide variety of seizure disorders. Partial seizures involve specific areas of the brain, and symptoms vary depending on the location of the seizure activity. Other seizures, called generalized seizures, involve a larger portion of the brain and usually cause uncontrolled movements of the entire body and loss of consciousness when they occur. Although the specific cause is unknown in many cases, epilepsy can be related to brain injury, tumors, or infections. The tendency to develop epilepsy may be genetic.

- **Head injuries.** Head injuries fit into two categories: external (usually scalp) injuries and internal head injuries. Internal injuries may involve the skull, the blood vessels within the skull, or the brain. Fortunately, most childhood falls or blows to the head result in injury to the scalp only, which is usually more frightening than threatening. An internal head injury could have more serious implications because the skull serves as the protective helmet for the delicate brain.

- **Concussions** are also a type of internal head injury. A concussion is the temporary loss of normal brain function as a result of an injury. Repeated concussions can result in permanent injury to the brain. One of the most common reasons kids get concussions is through sports, so it's important to make sure they wear appropriate protective head gear and don't continue to play if they've had a head injury.

- **Meningitis and encephalitis** are bacterial or viral infections of the brain and spinal cord. Meningitis is an inflammation of the coverings of the brain and spinal cord, and encephalitis is an inflammation of the brain tissue. Both conditions may result in permanent brain damage.

Benefits of infant massage on the nervous system:

- Infant massage can have a sedative or stimulating effect depending on the type of pressure and strokes given.

- Touch stimulates proprioceptive receptors of the skin which detect when an area of the body is out of its natural state and prompts the muscles to return the area to a resting state.

- The proprioceptive receptors along with the underlying tissue which help balance the autonomic nervous system, relax the muscles and help establish/re-establish proper muscle tone through its effect on the neuromuscular reflex pathways.

- Infant massage affects neurotransmitters of the brain and increases endorphin secretion, a natural painkiller.

- Infant massage can help reduce nerve entrapment through release of soft-tissue or muscular binding and reduce nerve root compression caused by muscular tension.

Musculoskeletal System

The musculoskeletal system consists of the skeleton (bones, cartilage, ligaments, and tendons) and its attached muscles. The skeleton and its attached muscles give the body basic structure and the ability for movement. In addition to their role in structure and movement, the larger bones in the body contain bone marrow, the site of production of blood cells. All bones serve as storage sites for calcium and phosphate.

As strong as bones are, they are capable of breaking. Muscles can weaken, and joints (as well as tendons, ligaments, and cartilage) can be damaged by injury or disease.

The following are common problems that can affect the bones, muscles, and joints in kids and teens:

- Arthritis is the inflammation of a joint that causes swelling, warmth, pain, and often trouble moving. Health problems that involve arthritis in kids and teens include juvenile rheumatoid arthritis (JRA), lupus, Lyme disease and septic arthritis—a bacterial infection of a joint.

  Benefits of infant massage on children with arthritis:

  – Research studies included children with mild to moderate juvenile rheumatoid arthritis who were massaged by their parents 15 minutes a day for 30 days (and a control group engaged in relaxation therapy: simple relaxation and breathing exercises). The findings at the end of the study were the children's anxiety and stress hormone (cortisol) levels were immediately decreased by the massage, and over the thirty day period their overall pain decreased on all of the following: self and parent pain reporting observations, their physician's assessment of pain (both the incidence and severity) and with pain-limiting activities.[11]

Resources:

  – The Official Patient's Sourcebook on Juvenile Rheumatoid Arthritis: A Revised and Updated Directory for the Internet Age by Icon Health Publications

- <u>Your Child with Arthritis: A Family Guide for Caregiving by Lori Tucker and Bethany DeNardo</u>

- <u>Raising a Child With Arthritis: A Parent's Guide, edited by the Arthritis Foundation</u>

- **Fractures** occur when a bone breaks; it may crack, snap, or shatter. After a bone fracture, new bone cells fill the gap and repair the break. Applying a strong plaster cast, which keeps the bone in the correct position until it heals, is the usual treatment. If the fracture is complicated, metal pins and plates can be placed to better stabilize the fracture while the bone heals.

- **Muscular dystrophy** is a genetic group of diseases that affect the muscles, causing them to weaken and break down over time. The most common form in childhood is called Duchenne muscular dystrophy, affecting predominately males.

- **Strains** occur when a muscle is overstretched. Strains usually happen when a person takes part in a strenuous activity when the muscles haven't properly warmed up or the muscle is not used to the activity (such as a new sport or playing a familiar sport after a long break).

- **Sprains** are an overstretching or a partial tear of the ligaments or tendons. Sprains are usually the result of an injury, such as twisting an ankle or knee. A common sprain injury is a torn Achilles tendon, which connects the calf muscles to the heel. This tendon can snap, but it usually can be repaired by surgery. Both strains and sprains are common in children and teens because they're active and still growing.

Benefits of infant massage on the muscular system:

- Infant massage helps reduce muscle and soft tissue pain by an increase in blood supply.

- Aids circulation for proper nutrition to the muscles.

- Helps muscles recover more quickly from exertion and fatigue by establishing and maintaining proper muscle tone.

- Encourages a higher metabolism and helps prevent muscular atrophy (wasting from specific health conditions, injury, or paralysis.)

- Relaxes the muscles, effectively reducing spasms, tension, and cramping.

- Infant massage reduces and breaks down adhesions (knots) in muscle tissue and stretches the connective tissue.

Benefits of infant massage on the skeletal system:

- Infant massage increases range of motion in joint movements increasing both the ease and efficiency of movement.

- Reduces strain and compression by releasing tight muscles and tendons.

- Helps increase the retention of nitrogen, phosphorus, and sulfur in the bones which aid in bone fracture healing and improving the circulation and overall nutrition in joints.

Respiratory System

The respiratory system includes the nose, nasopharynx, trachea, and lungs. The respiratory system brings oxygen from the air and excretes carbon dioxide and water back into the air.

The organs of the respiratory system are prone to a wide range of disorders caused by pollutants in our external environment: the air.

The most common problems of the respiratory system found in infants and children are:

- Asthma affects more than 20 million people in the United States. It's the number-one reason for kids chronically missing school. Asthma is a chronic inflammatory lung disease that causes airways to tighten and narrow. Often triggered by irritants in the air such as cigarette smoke, asthma flares involve contraction and swelling of the muscles lining the tiny airways. The resulting narrowing of the airways prevents air from flowing properly, causing wheezing and difficulty breathing, sometimes to the point of being life-threatening. Management of asthma starts with an asthma management plan, which usually involves avoiding asthma triggers and sometimes taking medications. An estimated 80 percent of kids with asthma develop symptoms by age 5, and 50 percent develop symptoms by age 2. It can be a frightening experience for both the parents and the child.

Benefits of infant massage on infants and children with asthma:

- Research studies showed very positive effects of parents massaging their asthmatic children, including increased peak air flow (a measure of the air pushed out of your child's lungs), improved pulmonary (lung) function, less anxiety and reduced stress hormone (cortisol) in the children massaged. Parental anxiety also decreased.12

Resources:

- www.EverydayKidz.com is a website devoted to children 1-8 years old with asthma that has a free program full of information and activities specifically designed to help asthma treatment become a non-frightening part of your child's asthma management routine.

- www.noattacks.org and www.noattacks.org/spanish (In Spanish.) Provide helpful tips for what you can do around your house to make it an asthma friendly environment by pointing out ways to prevent attacks by targeting and eliminating common irritants in your child's environment: mold, dust mites, second-hand smoke, cockroaches, cats and dogs, nitrogen dioxide and chemical irritants.

- Allergy and Asthma Network - Mothers of Asthmatics, 1-800-878-4403

- American Lung Association, 1-800-586-4872, www. lungusa.org/local visit this site to obtain phone numbers for local chapters.

- Asthma and Allergy Foundation of America, 1-800-727-8462, 7 a.m. - midnight

- EPA Resources - EPA provides free materials to help you learn more about controlling indoor asthma triggers. Visit www.epa.gov/asthma or call 1-800-438-4318 to order these free documents.

- *The Children's Hospital of Philadelphia Guide to Asthma: How to Help Your Child Live a Healthier Life* by Children's Hospital of Philadelphia.

- *The Complete Kid's Allergy and Asthma Guide: The Parent's Handbook for Children of All Ages* by Milton Gold

- **Bronchiolitis** (not to be confused with bronchitis) is an inflammation of the bronchioles, the smallest branches of the bronchial tree. Bronchiolitis affects mostly infants and young children, and can cause wheezing and serious difficulty breathing. It's usually caused by specific viruses in the wintertime, including respiratory syncytial virus (RSV).

- **Common cold** is caused by over 200 different viruses that cause inflammation in the upper respiratory tract. The common cold is the most common respiratory infection. Symptoms may include a mild fever, cough, headache, runny nose, sneezing, and sore throat.

- **Cough.** A cough is a symptom of an illness, not an illness itself. There are many different types of cough and many different causes, ranging from not-so-serious to life-threatening. Some of the more common causes affecting children are the common cold, asthma, sinusitis, seasonal allergies, croup, and pneumonia. Among the most serious causes of cough in children and adults are Tuberculosis (TB) and Pertussis (whooping cough).

- **Cystic fibrosis (CF)** affects more than 30,000 children and young adults in the United States, making CF the most common genetic disease affecting the lungs. Affecting primarily the respiratory and digestive systems, CF causes mucus in the body to be abnormally thick and sticky. The mucus can clog the airways in the lungs and make a person more vulnerable to bacterial infections.

To alter infant massage to assist in postural drainage, position baby with pillows under hips and back, positioning them at a 45-degree angle.

Children receiving daily bedtime massages from their parents reported being less anxious, and their mood and peak airflow (the measure of air pushed out of your child's lungs) readings improved.[19]

Resources:

- Cystic Fibrosis Foundation, 1-800-344-4823, http://www.cff.org Cystic Fibrosis-Reaching Out Foundation, Inc. 770-381-3710, info@ReachingOutFoundation.org , www.ReachingOutFoundation.org

- *Cystic Fibrosis: A Guide for Patient and Family* by David M. Orenstein

- *Cystic Fibrosis (It Happened to Me) The Ultimate Teen Guide* by Melanie Apel

- *Cystic Fibrosis: Everything You Need to Know (Your Personal Health)* by Wayne Kepron

- **Pneumonia** is an inflammation of the lungs that usually occurs from a bacterial or viral infection. Pneumonia causes fever, inflammation of lung tissue, and makes breathing difficult because the lungs have to work harder to transfer oxygen into the bloodstream and remove carbon dioxide from the blood.

Respiratory diseases common to newborns

Several respiratory conditions can affect a newborn baby just starting to breathe for the first time. Younger premature babies are at increased risk for conditions such as:

- **Respiratory distress syndrome of the newborn:** Babies born prematurely may not have enough surfactant in the lungs. Surfactant helps to keep the baby's alveoli open; without surfactant, the lungs collapse and the baby is unable to breathe.

- **Apnea of prematurity (AOP)** is a condition in which premature infants stop breathing for 15 to 20 seconds during sleep. Apnea of prematurity generally occurs after 2 days of life and up to a week of life. The lower the infant's weight and level of prematurity at birth, the more likely the child is to have AOP spells.

- **Bronchopulmonary dysplasia (BPD)** involves abnormal development of lung tissue. Sometimes called chronic lung disease or CLD, it's a disease in infants characterized by inflammation and scarring in the lungs. It develops most often in premature babies who are born with underdeveloped lungs.

Some other respiratory conditions of the newborn include:

- **Meconium aspiration** occurs when a newborn inhales (aspirates) a mixture of meconium (baby's first feces, ordinarily passed after birth) and amniotic fluid during labor and delivery. The inhaled meconium can cause a partial or complete blockage of the baby's airways.

- **Persistent pulmonary hypertension of the newborn (PPHN):** In the uterus, a baby's circulation bypasses the lungs. Normally, when a baby is born and begins to breathe air, his or her body quickly adapts and begins the process of respiration. PPHN occurs when a baby's body doesn't make the normal transition from fetal circulation to newborn circulation. This condition can cause symptoms such as rapid breathing, rapid heart rate, respiratory distress, and cyanosis (blue-tinted skin).

- **Transient tachypnea of the newborn (TTN):** Rapid breathing in a full-term newborn (more than 60 breaths a minute) is called transient tachypnea (pronounced: tah-kip-nee-uh).

Although some respiratory diseases and conditions can not be prevented, your child or teen can prevent many chronic lung and respiratory illnesses by avoiding smoking, staying away from pollutants and irritants, washing hands often to avoid infection, and getting regular medical checkups.

It is never too early to start talking to your kids about the dangers of smoking. Several websites have information to help you to motivate your children to stay tobacco-free: www.tobaccofree.org/children.html , www.notobacco.org , www.keepkidsfromsmoking.com

Benefits of infant massage with the respiratory system:

- Infant massage deepens and normalizes the breathing pattern through relaxation and release of tension in both the rib cage and diaphragm muscle, which are critical in inhalation and exhalation.

- Infant massage relieves congestion in the lungs, and increases the action of the heart, stimulating blood flow to and from the lungs. This helps eliminate carbon dioxide waste into the atmosphere and absorbing oxygen from the atmosphere into the blood.

Other Conditions that Benefit from Infant Massage

- Attention deficit hyperactivity disorder (ADHD) is thought to affect between 3 and 7 percent of the school age population in the US (2 million)ADHD is estimated to be 3-4 times more common in boys than girls. Children with ADHD showed more on-task behavior in the classroom and were rated as less hyperactive by their teachers following one month of twice-weekly massages.[13]

Resources:

- http://www.adhdnews.com/ provides support groups for families with children and adults with ADHD.

- http://www.add101.com/ is a website with a great base to begin learning about your child's ADHD diagnosis.

- *Power Parenting for Children with ADD/ADHD* by Grad L. Flick, PhD

- *The Gift of ADHD: How to Transform Your Child's Problems into Strengths* by Lara Honos-Webb

- *Taking Charge of ADHD: The Complete, Authoritative Guide for Parents* by Russell A. Barkley

- *Parenting Children With ADHD: 10 Lessons That Medicine Cannot Teach* (APA Lifetools) by Vincent Monastra, PhD

- **Autism:** Touch sensitivity, attention to sounds and off-task classroom behavior decreased and relatedness to teachers increased after massage therapy. Children in the massage group exhibited less stereotypic behavior and showed more on-task and social relatedness behavior during play observations at school, and they experienced fewer sleep problems at home.[14]

Resources:

- www.autismspeaks.org

- National Alliance for Autism Research, http://www.naar.org/ (888) 777-NAAR

- http://www.autisminfo.com/

- Autism Society of America www.autism-society.org

- AutismUSA.net Home Page www.autismusa.net

- Cure Autism Now (CAN) Home Page www.cureautismnow.org

- *Ten Things Every Child with Autism Wishes You Knew* by Ellen Notbohm

- *Autism Spectrum Disorders: The Complete Guide to Understanding Autism, Asperger's Syndrome, Pervasive Developmental Disorder, and Other ASDs* by Chantal Sicile-Kira and Temple Grandin

– *Thinking In Pictures: and Other Reports from My Life with Autism (Vintage)* by Temple Grandin

- **Cocaine (drug) exposed preterm newborns:** 85 percent of the newborns in one study were poly-drug exposed, meaning they had also been exposed to alcohol, marijuana and/or tobacco, however, cocaine was the primary drug reported. Massaged newborns had fewer postnatal complications, showed an average of 28 percent increased weight gain per day, better performance on the Brazelton Neonatal Behavior Assessment Scale particularly on the motor scale which helps the child inhibit random movements and control activity levels, letting the newborn focus her energy on other developmental tasks vital to growth. Newborns also showed less stress behaviors following 10 days of massage.18

Resources:

– Cocaine Anonymous- http://www.ca.org You can contact the C.A. World Services Office by phone 9:00 am to 5:00 pm, Monday through Friday (U.S. Pacific Time; GMT -0800) phone: 310-559-5833; International Referral Line at 1-800-347-8998. This number is a referral service for meeting information only. It is not a hotline.

– Chemically Dependent Anonymous: 1-888-CDA-HOPE; www.cdaweb.org

– SMART Recovery - Toll free: 866-951-5357 Tel: 440-951-5357 info@smartrecovery.com

– *Mothers, Babies, and Cocaine: The Role of Toxins in Development* by Michael Lewis

– *Joy Of Cocaine And Addiction Recovery: The Surrender And Resurrection Of The Soul* by Carlton Robinson

- **Down syndrome:** Infants with Down syndrome improved in muscle tone and in performance on motor tasks following massage therapy.[22]

Resources:

- National Down Syndrome Society, http://www.ndss.org/ 800- 221-4602

- A Directory of Websites dedicated to Down Syndrome: http://www.downsyndrome.com/

- *Babies with Down Syndrome: A New Parent's Guide* (The Special Needs Collection) by Karen Stray-Gundersen.

- *A Parent's Guide to Down Syndrome: Toward a Brighter Future, Revised Edition* by Siegfried Pueschel

- *Early Communication Skills for Children With Down Syndrome: A Guide for Parents and Professionals* by Libby Kumin

- Psychiatric patients (child and adolescent): After five 30-minute massages, children and adolescents had better sleep patterns, lower depression and anxiety and lower stress hormone levels (cortisol and norepinephrine).[26]

See *Managing Children with Psychiatric Problems* by M. Elena Garralda

- Spinal cord injuries: Massage therapy improved functional abilities, range of motion, and muscle strength in spinal cord injury patients.[27]

Resources:

- National Spinal Cord Injury Association - http://www. spinalcord.org/

- The Christopher and Dana Reeve Paralysis Resource Center (PRC) 1-800-539-7309 http://www.paralysis.org

- *Spinal Cord Injury: A Guide for Living* by Sara Palmer

- *From There to Here: Stories of Adjustment to Spinal Cord Injury* by Gary Karp

- *Still Me,* and *Nothing is Impossible: Reflections on a New Life* by Christopher Reeve

Tips on Sharing the News of a Disability or Disease with Family and Friends

Sandra McElwee of Santa Margarita, California added a note to her son Sean's birth announcement (who was born with Down Syndrome) encouraging people how to respond:

"Dear Family and Friends,

> Sean is a very special baby, and the birth announcement can't possibly say it all. God has made Sean special and chosen us to be his parents... we feel blessed. Sean was born with Down syndrome. We want to give you time to adjust to the news, so you wouldn't feel the need to have an immediate response. We hope you will feel the same as we do. We're happy and proud. We would like you to see him as we do: a beautiful baby boy. We also want you to treat him just like any other baby and congratulate us. We have a baby. We're a family now. This is not a sad moment; please do not apologize, as we aren't sorry. We are still gathering information on Down syndrome and probably won't be able to answer any questions for awhile. We would like to encourage you to call us and come to see Sean. He sleeps, eats, cries, and dirties diapers just like every other baby. He just has an extra chromosome."

Where can I look for Support for Special Needs Babies or More Information?

Your pediatrician or local hospital should be able to point you towards support groups. If you have computer access, you can go to www.google.

com and enter your child's specific condition, along with keywords such as: national, foundation, and/or support and see what your search engine comes up with. If you don't have access at home to a computer you can utilize your local library's resources, computer online articles, and hard-copy books on their shelves.

Looking for information on a rare disorder? Contact:

- The National Organization for Rare Disorders (NORD), at 1-800-999-6673, and: www.rarediseases.org

- The Office of Rare Disorders at the National Institutes of Health, at: http://rarediseases.info.nih.gov/index.html

- The Genetic and Rare Diseases Information Center, which is a part of the Office of Rare Disorders and which answers questions from the general public, including patients and their families, health care professionals and biomedical researchers. Call toll-free at: 1-888-205-2311 (Voice), 1-888-205-3223 (TTY).

- DiseaseInfoSearch, for information on specific genetic conditions, at: www.geneticalliance.org/DIS/

- Contact NICHCY (http://www.nichcy.org/ or 800-695-0285 or nichcy@aed.org), for the *National Dissemination Center for Children with Disabilities.* The center serves the nation as a central source of information on:

    – Disabilities in infants, toddlers, children, and youth

    – IDEA, which is the law authorizing special education

    – No Child Left Behind (as it relates to children with disabilities)

    – Research-based information on effective educational practices

        NICHCY has a one-stop resource searching across a spectrum of health and disability conditions: www.nichcy.org/resources/galore.asp#health

43

There are numerous sites that provide medically based information about health conditions and disabilities. The site has listed them under a separate A-Z page, but you can quickly go there (the link above will take you) and search to your heart's content.

Specific disability information can also be found online at: www. accessunlimited.com

Contraindications to Infant Massage

If your baby has any health condition, disease or disorder, please consult with your pediatrician before starting any of the infant massage strokes in this book. In addition, please do not massage an infant with: acute infection, fever, staph infection, tuberculosis, hemophilia, high blood pressure, contagious skin disorder, inflammation, fractures, osteoporosis, distention of abdomen or abdominal lump, nausea, vomiting, diarrhea, swollen joints, malignant cysts, jaundice, recent surgery, advanced stage diabetes, gastrointestinal or jejunostomy feeding tubes at least two weeks after surgery or until healed, varicose veins, dislocated or broken bones, hydrocephalus (don't massage around the shunt) and seizure disorders.

If your child has any of the above-listed conditions, please consult with your child's pediatrician or occupational or physical therapist on how to tailor the massage strokes to your child, along with when and whether it is harmful to your child *prior* to beginning any infant massage with your child. If your baby is in the NICU, please consult with the nurse or doctor assigned to your baby as to what touch is appropriate. He or she will take into consideration your child's age, weight, and overall health status. Preterm babies and infants in the NICU need special care—please see Chapter Three.

Chapter Three: Benefits of Infant Massage to Premature Babies and Infants in the Newborn Intensive Care Unit (NICU) and Adjustments to Infant Massage Routine

Newborns who are placed in the newborn intensive care unit (NICU) of a hospital are exposed to many different stimuli, including high-intensity sporadic noise such as alarms and bright lights, cold, and invasive and often painful procedures. Newborns in a study responded well to touch intervention (still touch techniques and/or infant massage.) Those infants who were receiving touch were associated with fewer startle responses, decreased need for ventilation, and even fewer clenched fists.

Preterm infants who were massaged before sleep fell asleep more quickly and slept more soundly, with better sleep patterns. They showed improved weight gain after only five days and up to 21 percent after receiving 3, 15 minutes massages for 10 days, as compared to infants who were not massaged before sleep. Those infants who received infant massage were awake and active for a greater period of time and scored higher on the Brazelton Scale.

What Can Infant Massage Mean to Your Baby in The NICU When it Comes to Medical Cost?

Preterm infants who received infant massage, gained an average of 47 percent more weight, became more socially responsive, and were discharged six days earlier, at a hospital cost savings of $10,000 per infant (or $4.7 billion dollars if the 470,000 preemies born each year were massaged).

Although the underlying mechanism for this relationship between infant massage and weight gain has not yet been clinically established, possibilities that have been explored in studies with both humans and rats include increased protein synthesis, increased vagal (vagus nerve, a cranial nerve that senses aortic blood pressure, slows heart rate, and stimulates digestive organs and taste) activity that releases hormones like insulin (food absorption hormone) and enhances gastric motility (muscular contractions of the intestines) and decreased cortisol (stress hormone) levels leading to increased oxytocin, which may also have significance for uterine contraction, lactation, and mother-infant interaction.[10]

Adjustments to the Basic Infant Massage Routine for Premature Babies and Infants in the NICU

Infants in the NICU need special handling and care. Please talk with your infant's nurse or doctor before applying any of the infant massage techniques to your infant. Find out what drugs your infant has been given; some drugs such as Curare and Pavulon (both common muscle relaxants used in the NICU,) will make your baby unresponsive to the massage. Even then, your touch is important as your baby can see, hear, and feel you.

After first learning how to correctly scrub up and garb yourself in hospital gowns, before visiting your baby in the NICU, you may be shocked by the number of machines and instruments applied to your child. Try to find comfort in knowing that your premature infant has a significantly greater chance of surviving now than ever before, due to these medical advancements.

At a minimum, your infant will be warmed and monitored with equipment that includes:

- Cardiorespiratory monitor to keep track of your infant's heart rate and breathing.

- Isolette, which is the heater.

- Pulse oximeter to keep track of the oxygen level in your infants blood.

- Temperature probe to keep track of your infant's body temperature.

If your infant has additional medical needs, equipment also may be used, including, but not limited to:

- Continuous positive airway pressure (CPAP), for help with breathing (during periods of mild to moderate apnea from prematurity, mild lung problems or when being weaned from a ventilator.

- Intravenous (IV) site which may be moved daily, to administer fluid, medication and for feeding.

- Transcutaneous oxygen and/or carbon dioxide monitor to measure levels constantly without use of a needle.

- Umbilical catheter, for administering fluid, for feeding, and medication.

- Ventilator for help with breathing.

Unless your newborn is very sick or immature, you will be allowed to touch and hold him or her. Your infant's nurse or doctor will show you how to work around the technology and to alert you to your infant's special needs. If your nurse or doctor in the NICU gives you the go-ahead on infant massage, follow the following adjustments to the infant massage routine provided in this book:

- Verbally tell your child you are about to begin massaging him or her. Apply a dime-size amount of oil into the palm of your hands and rub them together to warm the oil.

- Follow the techniques listed below, being careful to move around any tubes, gauze, monitors, or other items that may be attached to your baby. You should have a member of the NICU staff or a Certified Infant Massage Instructor assist you, especially the first few times until you are familiar with the routine.

It is most important in the NICU to remember infant stress cues. Infant stress cues indicate that your infant needs to be withdrawn from infant massage due to over-stimulation. Examples of infant stress cues are: Apnea (momentary stop in breathing), bradycardia (which signals reduced heart rate, which the monitors in the NICU will signal), a rapid heart beat (tachycardia), drop in oxygen levels (oxygen desaturation), skin mottling (vascular changes that cause a patchy appearance), hiccups, and gagging. Even a subtle sign, such as looking away from you while you speak or make eye contact is a common, infant stress cue.

If your baby shows these signs, give the baby time to rest, then use a still touch technique. If your infant still displays stress cues, let him or her rest and try again later. Please see Chapter Five for instruction on Kangaroo Care and still touch techniques if you or your NICU staff member decides your infant isn't ready to receive infant massage.

Infant Massage Routine for Newborns in the NICU

The following sequence should be repeated three times daily for optimum results. Still touch or the kangaroo hold may be incorporated before and/or after or in replacement of this routine.

For each area the strokes should be applied at a slightly firm touch. Practice pressure with your nurse before applying to your infant. Each stroke should last about five seconds, in the direction of the heart, and you should apply about 10 strokes per section.

1. Begin by holding your baby with your hands gently on their sides, cupping them for a few moments and letting them know verbally you are going to begin a massage.

2. With the baby lying either over your shoulder, across your lap or in a football hold in an arm, stroke the top of their head down to their neck.

3. From the bottom of the neck go across the shoulders, back and forth.

4. From the upper back, glide down to the waist, repeat.

5. Hip to foot on one leg, 10 strokes, then the other leg.

6. Hand to shoulder on one arm, 10 strokes, then the other arm.

Chapter Four: Setting the Stage—Preparing for Your First Infant Massage, Non-verbal Communication, and Benefits of Jojoba Massage Oil and Aromatherapy for Infants

The best time to introduce massage is anytime from birth through pre-crawling stage, as it will be easiest to keep your baby in position for the massage. However, you can begin infant massage with babies and children of any age by just applying the strokes to them in the position that works for them, which may be in a variety of different positions, as most post-crawling and walking babies won't lie down for the duration of the massage. In a study, even preschool children who had received massage fell asleep sooner and slept longer during nap time and had decreased activity levels and better behavior ratings.

Although there is no best time of day for a massage, many parents make a routine with using infant massage before laying the baby down for sleep, perhaps after an evening bath, as the massage itself has proven to help increase the duration of sleep in infants to become longer and sounder.

Before beginning any massage on your infant, you will want to set up a safe area for your little one. You will need a towel rolled up lengthwise and folded in a horseshoe shape with the opening towards you, a waterproof pad or cloth diaper underneath your baby, a bottle of organic oil (out of baby's reach) and a blanket to swaddle your baby in to keep him or her warm after the massage. Make sure you have dim lighting and a warm room for the massage so the baby is comfortable. You may need to use a small portable room heater.

In the background, you may want to play soft classical music or other sounds you and baby find soothing, such as a natural landscapes CD with waterfall, a heartbeat, or mother's womb recording on repeat if you have those available. You may want to turn off the ringer on your phone and/or remove any distractions before the massage, begins in order to ensure you can fully concentrate on your baby from start until finish once you have started.

Position the baby where she is comfortable, with her neck resting on the towel, on the end of the upside-down U. Have your baby facing you so that when you lean over the baby you are within 7-15" inches of the baby, so she can see you clearly. Your baby is programmed to search out the human face, searching out the contrasting bull's eye shape of the eye. This will allow your baby to shut down the production of stress hormones and begin to relate relaxation to not only your touch but your face as well. After your baby reaches eight months, sight becomes normal and she will easily be able to see you at any sitting distance, although close is always best for bonding.

In study after study, the human face with its contrasting areas of light and dark have gone up against the most bold and colorful prints and patterns, and time and time again has solely emerged as the object that holds the infant's attention longest. Keep eye contact and talk or sing to your baby during the massage.

If your baby is five months or under and still has the tonic neck reflex that causes him or her to look off to the side, you can sit with your legs open in a circle with your knees out to the sides and your soles coming together, positioning your baby with the head supported on the soles of your feet, rather than using a towel. However you can position yourself and your baby so that you both are comfortable and safe is best for your infant massage routine.

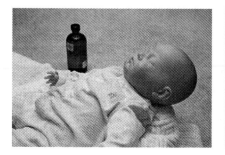 

In your home, you can undo the diaper fasteners or massage without the diaper when you need to access the lower back, hip, and buttocks. A cloth diaper or waterproof pad may be placed under your baby in case of any accidents. You can also use a cloth diaper to "tent" the genital area if you are massaging a baby boy, to avoid accidents while massaging the lower back, hip, and buttocks.

Please keep in mind, finish time is always up to the baby and will vary with each massage. In time, you will come to recognize when your baby does not want a massage or is finished early when you become more comfortable with your baby's non-verbal cues.

How to Communicate With Your Infant through Non-verbal Cues and Baby Sign Language (ASL)

When born and throughout the first year of life, your infant has a desire to communicate her needs and wishes with her caretaker but lacks the ability to do so clearly. Infants can only express themselves through non-verbal cues such as crying, eye contact, gestures, vocal sounds, facial expressions, touching, watching, reaching, body movement, anticipation, smiling, etc. This can lead to frustration and temper tantrums in children of all ages.

Infant massage provides a great opportunity to listen, observe, and learn your child's specific non-verbal cues to ease the frustration of your child who is desperately trying to communicate her needs and wishes with you.

The hand-eye coordination required for sign language develops sooner than the coordination required for speech in the parent's language (the lips, tongue, breath, and vocal cords need to be developed simultaneously with learning a huge vocabulary). By using simple signs for common words in the infant's environment, such as "eat," "drink," "sleep," "more," "hug," "play," "massage," "bath," etc., infants can learn to express their needs before they are physically capable of producing comprehensible speech.

Baby sign became popular when studies showed that when babies born into deaf families, whether the babies themselves were deaf or hearing, were immersed in a complete signing environment, they were able to use simple signs from as early as six weeks. It has been estimated that 90 percent of a baby's linguistic observations are observations of interactions between others, not interactions between himself or herself and others.

Infants naturally desire to use the communication form they are immersed in, and use of sign among other family members is at least as important as use of sign to the baby. If early use of sign language is desired, use sign for the words you are trying to teach with each other in front of the baby. The baby will also need to spend some time in actual instruction.

To begin to teach a specific sign—for example, "eat"— you use the sign and the verbal "eat," repeatedly in a sentence. For example, "Chloe, it is time to eat (use sign) lunch. Chloe, do you want to eat (use sign) lunch now? Mommy is hungry too, let's eat! (use sign)." Repetition is key for learning. (Do the actual sign when you say the word it represents.)

In the medical field, baby sign is highly recommended for infants, toddlers, and children with developmental delays and speech difficulties due to physical disabilities other than hearing impairment by speech and occupational therapists. Infants with speech difficulties due to physical disabilities will often have the mental ability necessary for language development and are only hampered by skeletal, muscular, or other limiting problems, such as hypertonia common in many disorders. Baby sign instruction will allow those babies to express themselves despite their disabilities.

I encourage all parents of well, preterm and babies with disabilities to take a baby sign class with www.LittleLocalCelebrity.com (Maryland, D.C., and Northern Virginia residents) or with www.KinderWorkShops.com (US) at any age from birth on. General benefits of baby sign are that it will enable pre-verbal children to communicate their wants and needs, accelerate communication and results in earlier verbal language, enhance receptive and expressive vocabulary, reduce frustration, enhance receptive and expressive vocabulary, make learning to read easier, enhance creative ability, and result in a higher IQ by 10-12 points!

By the time your child is 18-35 months old, he or she can sign two- to four-word sentences and thus communicate with you with less frustration. Studies suggest that hearing children who sign as infants go on to develop particularly rich spoken vocabularies, as well as a tendency to solve problems through communication rather than tantrums. They may also teach sign to younger siblings after they themselves have switched to speaking with their parents.

Here are some basic signs to help you communicate with your baby, all taken from American Sign Language (ASL). Remember, make the sign while you say the word it represents.

- To sign "massage," (using American Sign Language or ASL): Tap shoulders with both hands (right hand taps right shoulder and left hand taps left shoulder with fingertips at the same time,) then with each hand make a thumbs up sign and with knuckles facing each other and thumbs up, push thumbs down as if massaging, and verbally say, "massage." To use this in a sentence you could say, "Chloe, do you want Mommy to give you a (sign and say) 'massage'?" Then follow up with still hold to begin the massage. Photos are available at: www.LittleLocalCelebrity.com

- To sign "hug/love": With arms at sides, pull them up and into a tight x, crossing wrists and pulling in as if hugging something, your shoulders also move in with the action. To use this in a sentence you could say, "Chloe do you want Mommy to (sign and say) 'hug' you?" Then give your child a long, loving hug.

- To sign "more," face your wrists and palms together, bend your wrist at a 90-degree angle and in towards each other so that when you touch all your fingertips in together, they are facing each other, tap them together and say "more." To use this in a sentence you could say, "Chloe, would you like (sign and say) 'more' massage on your feet?" or, "Chloe, would you like (sign and say) 'more' milk?"

Make sure you use repetition and let your baby imitate your words when you make each sign; this is a very important step in communication, allowing your child to begin to relate words to objects and actions important in her daily life. You can point and look at the object which will begin to signal you child that their attention should look in that direction. Babies as young as 42 minutes old have been observed imitating their parent's facial expressions—even sticking out their tongues, suggesting neonatal comprehension, very early on.

Tips on Comforting Your Baby

So you've gotten your setup ready for a massage but your little one isn't on the same wavelength. Here are some ideas to help soothe your little one:

Fussing and crying is a natural and very necessary part of early communication. It lets us know that the baby needs something: food, entertainment, or sleep; or that he or she is in pain, among other things. It is innate to want to console a crying infant. Nursing mothers, upon hearing an infant's cry, actually release a chemical triggering the let-down response. Even one-day old infants became distressed at the cry of another newborn baby, but not that of an older baby or synthesized sound.

When babies fuss and cry, it is culturally imposed that we must hush our baby, that the mother is doing something wrong. Try letting go of your preconceived notions on crying or what other people are thinking and respond appropriately, to what you think your baby needs. Here are some ideas you may use to console your little one:

- Baby in Motion. Gently bounce up and down or sway your baby from side to side. Many new parents use their fitness balls to bounce on while holding an infant over their shoulder, on their belly, or across their lap. Vibrating bouncy seats and swings also work wonders. The "vestibular motion" mimics the feeling your baby had in your womb. You can try driving your baby around the block, which has a dual feature of providing steady motion and white noise. Never shake your baby.

- Music. Gentle, rhythmic melodies, whether a lullaby, classical music, African drums, soundscapes (rain, the ocean tide,) recordings of a mother's heartbeat or womb, or of a parent's humming are all ways to distract and comfort your baby. If you can get in the habit of singing or humming your baby to sleep, try to use that same song to comfort her. She will recall and start to connect it to instant relaxation while she quickly nods off.

- White noise makers. Turn on the vacuum, running water, or a fan. A baby's neurological system isn't able to tune out stimulating environmental sounds; white noise may be such the distractor your baby is searching for.

- Distraction. Go for a walk in the stroller, a ride in the car, shake a rattle, read a book, sing while you practice the post-partum tandem exercises for mother and baby found in Chapter Ten; anything that will captivate your little one and distract him or her.

- Crying it out. Sometimes, it is best to just hold them, rock them in a rocking chair, or put them in their crib or playpen and let them cry until they fall asleep. Sometimes your baby may just be over-stimulated and needs to be held or rocked gently and allowed to cry out the tension. It is not recommended to let an infant under three months sit and cry it out alone, but it is okay to sit with her, holding her and waiting 5 to 10 minutes to see if she just needs some time to release pent-up frustration. With an older baby, you may place her in the crib for up to 15 minutes to see if what she really needs is a nap. You need to provide the opportunity for her to soothe herself on occasion.

Sometimes your infant may not be in the mood to receive infant massage. If she expresses this, just wait it out and try again later, or the following day. If she is fussy when you begin, try the still touch on her legs to begin with and only massage that part for a few days. Slowly increase the massage routine to other parts in order to build a tolerance to massage. If your infant is still exhibiting stress cues with the still touch, let her sleep and try again at a later time.

Oils Used for Massage

In a study, infants showed fewer stress behaviors (e.g., grimacing and clenched fists) and lower cortisol levels (stress hormones) following massage with oil versus massage without oil.[34] The skin is the largest organ of our body; it is our first line of defense protecting us against chemicals, dirt, germs and pollution found in our everyday life.

Our skin also serves as a delicate filtering system, allowing only select substances to enter our bloodstream (as an example, think of the many medications that are administered transdermally, or through the skin, such as hormones and nicotine), and helps us eliminate toxins from our systems. Babies and children have delicate, sensitive skin, newly exposed to the ferocities of our everyday environment, so it's especially important to consider what products we use on them. Babies and children also love to put their hands (feet and everything!) in their mouths, so remember that any moisturizers, powders, oils, or lotions may be ingested by your child. It's important to make sure that the oils, lotions, soaps, creams, and powders that we use on children are as natural, healthy, and safe as possible.

Why is Mineral Oil Not Recommended for Infant Massage?

Most baby lotions and oils we use have key ingredients of mineral oil. Mineral oil is also found in other forms as: petrolatum, paraffin oil or wax, propylene glycol, or other petroleum products. Mineral oil is also a non-renewable resource; it is the leftover liquid hydrocarbons, of the distillation of gasoline from crude oil. It is very abundant, making it extremely inexpensive—it is actually more expensive to dispose of mineral oil than to purchase it!

Unfortunately, mineral oil is an unnatural product that acts similar to a thin plastic coating over the skin, suffocating the breathing process of our cells, inhibiting a main purpose of the skin, which is to take in oxygen from the environment and release carbon dioxide. Mineral oil does not absorb well into the skin, and actually clogs pores, which makes it difficult for our skin to eliminate toxins. Mineral oil may actually produce symptoms similar to dry skin, interfering with the natural moisturizing process of the skin by absorbing the skin's natural oils, thus increasing skin dehydration—contrary to its main purpose for use.

Adelle Davis, in her book, "Let's Eat Right to Keep Fit," writes that she "personally would be afraid to use this oil even in baby oils, cold creams, or other cosmetics." Due to all the harmful effects of mineral oil on a baby's system, it is best to use all natural ingredients. Oils that are all-natural, vegetable- or fruit-based, and/or organic are best to use. These natural oils will be easily absorbed and when they are digested transdermally will actually benefit your child. Oils with vitamin E, for example, will benefit the skin by acting as an antioxidant. If your child has eczema, acne, or diaper rash, avoid oils with colorants and fragrances as they may only worsen the condition. All-natural products are the safest things to use on our children.

WARNING: Mineral (baby) oil contains hydrocarbons that can be deadly. If children aspirate (inhale) baby oil, their lungs become coated with the oil. This blocks oxygen and prevents proper respiration, ultimately leading to chemical pneumonia. To keep little hands from opening baby oil bottles, store baby oil where your child can't reach it. For further safety, childproof caps on baby oil bottles have been made mandatory since October 2002. However, even childproof lids are not always childproof: my daughter easily removed them at as young as 12 months old! She removed lids on many containers in under a minute, so please be sure to keep them out of reach of your little ones at all times![35]

Why Jojoba Oil is best for Infant Massage

When choosing an oil for my line, "Little Local Celebrity Organic Massage Oil" (See www.LittleLocalCelebrity.com), I chose 100 percent organic Jojoba (pronounced ho-ho-ba) oil. It is very similar to the natural oil our skin produces, though it is technically a liquid wax produced from the seed of the Jojoba simmondsia chinensis shrub. For centuries, the desert of the American Southwest held a secret known only to the indigenous people who lived there. Their secret was a scrubby little bush with an amazing seed. When this seed bean was roasted it secreted oil that was as much a medicine as it was a moisturizer. This rich extract helps the jojoba desert plant retain water during the long summer drought. It acts as a humectant and creates a protective film over the skin and hair shaft that helps keep moisture in.

Jojoba oil is naturally moisturizing, healing, and beneficial for all skin types. The best claim to fame for Jojoba oil is that it has been accepted as a substitute for sperm whale oil, formerly often used in the manufacture of cosmetics. The similarity to our natural sebum (oil) helps it penetrate the skin easily. It is great for acne prone skin as it can both mix with our natural sebum and dissolve sebum, and also can unclog pores making it a great oil for use on the face.

The oil has a profound effect on cuts and sores, and when applied to the skin it moisturizes and softens it. Jojoba oil is recognized to fight wrinkles in the skin, helps rejuvenates the skin, promotes new cell growth, and contains anti-bacterial properties. Plus, it does not go rancid, making it great for aromatherapy.

Jojoba oil has four different grades that are produced, 1-4, 1 being the highest. My line is made with the best, grade 1: a pure, natural golden color that has not been bleached, decolorized, deodorized, or distilled. This grade has a very slight, pleasant aroma that is distinct to Jojoba oil. Besides all the great benefits of Jojoba oil, our Jojoba oil is 100 percent Organic!

Why it's worth it to pay extra for Organic

When choosing whether or not to go organic with my "Little Local Celebrity Organic Massage Oil," I chose to go organic, because 100 percent organic Jojoba oil is produced without the use of artificial pesticides, herbicides, and genetically modified organisms (GMOs). It's really "natural," and natural is best, and it's that simple.

The United States Department of Agriculture has very strict legal definitions for products which call themselves natural and/or organic. Their definition of "natural" is: a product containing no artificial ingredient or added color and that is only minimally processed (a process which does not fundamentally alter the raw product) may be labeled natural. The label must explain the use of the term natural (e.g., no added colorings or artificial ingredients and minimally processed). However, in order for a product to call itself organic in the United States, several strict, specific criteria must be met.

Labeling products as organic is a valuable marketing label in today's economy. Today's health-conscious consumers understand that organic products have the following attributes: avoidance of synthetic (manmade) chemical inputs such as certain fertilizers, pesticides, antibiotics, food additives, and genetically modified organisms along with the use of farmland that has been free from chemicals for a number of years (often, three); keeping detailed written production and sales records (audit trail); maintaining strict physical separation of organic products from non-certified products; and undergoing periodic on-site inspections.

In the United States, to protect consumers from companies that misuse the word "organic," federal organic legislation clearly defines three different levels of "organic," of which the first two can display the USDA organic seal signifying 95 percent or more organic material. The first category contains only products made entirely with certified organic ingredients and methods which can be labeled "100 percent organic." The second category contains products with 95 percent organic ingredients, which can use the word "organic." A third category, containing a minimum of 70 percent organic ingredients, can be labeled "made with organic ingredients." In addition, all three levels of organic products may also display the logo of the certification body that approved them. In the United States, products made with less than 70 percent organic ingredients cannot advertise themselves as "organic" at all to consumers on their label; they can only mention this fact in the product's ingredient statement.

100 percent Organic Jojoba Oil, "Little Local Celebrity Organic Massage Oil," can be purchased at my site: www.LittleLocalCelebrity.com in both unscented and scented, which is infused with Lavender and/or Chamomile essential oil. The scented versions are only for use on infants three months and older.

Aromatherapy (Essential Oil) Application and Benefits for Infants and Children

Aromatherapy, meaning "treatment using scent," is ancient art of the use of plant essences, also known as essential oils, to relieve discomforts of physical ailments and promote emotional well being, as well as cognitive development in babies. Aromatherapy can be a wonderful addition to your infant massage routine.

Even small babies as young as three months can enjoy the therapeutic effects of essential oils. It is not recommended to use essential oils on babies younger than three months old. They are still developing in many ways and are adjusting to life outside the womb. Essential oils are too strong in most instances to use at this stage.

Essential aromatherapy safety information:

- Essential oils are highly concentrated liquids that can be harmful if not used carefully. Implementing aromatherapy into your lifestyle shouldn't cause paranoia or undue worry. By treating essential oils as herbal medicines and following the steps outlined below, you will be well on your way to safely enjoying the many benefits that aromatherapy can offer.

- Always make sure you are using only pure, natural essential oils, as fragrance oils or other synthetic oils have no healing properties. Use only half the amount of essential oils when dealing with children that you would use for an adult. For babies up to two years old up to a 1 percent dilution is recommended (up to 5 drops essential oil to 1 ounce or 2 tablespoons massage oil). After two years up to a 2 percent dilution may be used (up to 10 drops essential oil to 1 ounce or 2T carrier oil).

- Dilute all essential oils before applying topically (to the skin). Use only the smallest amount needed. Do not apply undiluted essential oils, absolutes, CO_2s, or other concentrated essences onto the skin. Although lavender and tea tree oil may be used undiluted on the skin by experienced aromatherapy practitioners, on rare occurrences a severe sensitivity may arise, so please never use any essential oil undiluted.

- If you are uncomfortable mixing the oils into your massage oils, there are several methods of application that are suitable for use with babies and children such as applying a few drops of essential oil to a tissue or handkerchief and waving it several inches in front of the child's nose, so it can be inhaled or by adding it to a diffuser.

- If you are pregnant, avoid: angelica, aniseed, basil, camphor, hyssop, jasmine, juniper, lovage, peppermint, rosemary, savory, and sage essential oils. If you or your child have epilepsy or any disease, disorder, or condition of the central nervous system, avoid fennel, hyssop, sage, wormwood, and rosemary essential oils. If you or your child suffers from any other medical condition such as asthma, liver damage, cancer, or have any other medical problem, use oils only under the proper guidance of your physician and/or a qualified and trained aromatherapy practitioner before using oils with your child.

- Do not take any oils internally without consultation from a qualified aromatherapy practitioner. Use extreme caution when using oils with children and give children only the gentlest oils at extremely low doses. It is safest to consult a qualified aromatherapy practitioner before using oils with children. Keep oils away from children and out of the way of fire hazards as they are flammable.

Skin patch test:

A skin patch test should be conducted prior to using new massage oil for the first time to avoid sensitization or an allergic reaction. Place a small amount of the diluted essential oil (never use essential oils undiluted on the skin) on the inside of your elbow and apply a bandage. Wait 24-48 hours to see if there is any form of reaction. Even if a particular essential oil is not known to cause irritation, this step should not be ignored. Even if an oil does not irritate you, it still can irritate someone else. It is important that you always keep that in mind.

There are several safe essential oils that can provide relief for many baby ailments. Below is a list of common essential oils, with their botanical name following their common name in parentheses, that are recommended for babies and children by age appropriate for use, and their therapeutic benefits; this list is educational only, please consult with your pediatrician prior to using any essential oil with your child:

For babies under three months: Unscented oil, such as "Little Local Celebrity Organic Massage Oil," (www.LittleLocalCelebrity.com) should be used—do not add any essential oils.

For babies three months and older: Some scented oils may be used—lavender and chamomile scented, or a combination of lavender and chamomile (available in an organic Jojoba oil carrier oil at www.LittleLocalCelebrity.com).

- Roman chamomile (*Anthemis nobilis*) essential oil distilled from the dried flowers of the chamomile plant produced mainly in Italy, has a crisp, slightly fruity and herbaceous scent, giving your baby a sense of peace. It cools his or her skin and soothes the digestive system. It has been used as a calming remedy for children for decades as an antiseptic, analgesic, anti-inflammatory, and skin-soothing agent with anti-oxidation and antispasmodic qualities. It's helpful for teething pain, infantile colic, and calming overly tired children (or adults with insomnia) because it tends to produce a restful sleep with deep relaxation and tranquility.

- **Lavender** (*Lavendula officinalis),* essential oil distilled from the flower heads of the lavender plant that is produced in Europe with its floral, herbaceous, slightly fruity scent, takes its name from the Latin word *lavare,* meaning "to wash." Lavender possesses a clean, pure aroma. It encourages balance for the entire nervous system and is helpful for infantile colic and helps treat thrush. Lavender benefits every body system.

Lavender stimulates the production of gastric juices and bile, aids digestion, and increases intestinal mobility in the digestive system where it is used to treat dyspepsia, flatulence, colic, nausea, and diarrhea. It stimulates the production of urine, restores hormonal balance, reduces cramps in the urinary/reproductive system, and is used to treat infections, leucorrhea, and cystitis. It lowers blood pressure and also to ease hypertension in the circulatory system.

Lavender reduces muscular tension, relieves pain and is used to treat muscular aches, rheumatism, lumbago, and sprains in the muscular system. In the respiratory system it acts as an antiseptic and antispasmodic, used for throat infections, flu, bronchitis, whooping cough, asthma, sinus congestion, laryngitis, and tonsillitis.

In the skin, it is a wonderful antiseptic, controlling the production of sebum and stimulating circulation in the skin. It assists in the healing of wounds (aids in the formation of scar tissue) and helps to rejuvenate the skin. For burns in children, you can add lavender essential oil (1-2 drops) into a bowl, mix with very cold water and use as a cloth compress to lay over burns. Lavender is commonly used to treat acne, cuts, burns, sunburn, inflammation, psoriasis, and wrinkles.

For the nervous system it is calming, refreshing, and relaxing, used to treat depression, headache, insomnia, headache, nervous exhaustion, restlessness, and moodiness. It clears the head and increases mental alertness. It is also used to treat insect bites and stings, and to repel moths.

For babies six months and older:

- Geranium (*Pelargonium graveolens),* with its strong floral, slightly fruity scent, can restore balance to oily or dry hair and skin and is gentle enough for sensitive skin. Effective as a natural insecticide due to its terpine content, it is used to repel ticks, fleas, and mosquitoes from humans and animals alike. It can also be used in the treatment of lice and ringworm and as a mild analgesic and sedative to treat minor pain felt in the nervous system. It is not for use in women during pregnancy; however, for women in menopause, it can be used to balance the production of androgens (hormones) by stimulating the adrenal cortex. Due to immune-stimulating properties of geranium, it's not advised for use on anyone who has an autoimmune disease.

- Mandarin (*Citrus reticulata)* has a relaxing, cheerful, sweet and fruity citrus scent that is very uplifting and invigorating. It has benefits for acne, dull skin, insomnia, oily skin, scars, spots, stress, stretch marks, scars, and wrinkles. Mandarin is good to use on a child that is easily over-excited or to calm frequent temper-tantrums. During pregnancy, it can be used to boost circulation and discourage water retention. There is some evidence that mandarin essential oil is photo-toxic, reacts strongly to sunlight, and can cause sensitivities. Direct sunlight, such as sunbathing or tanning beds, should be avoided after using the mandarin essential oil.

- Neroli (*Citrus aurantium)* is named after an Italian princess of Nerola who wore the oil of this flower as a perfume— this oil is certainly fit for your little prince and/or princess!

Neroli has many benefits for use with depression, digestive problems, dry or sensitive skin, flatulence, headaches, insomnia, irritable bowel syndrome, stress, and panic attacks. Neroli has antispasmodic properties and should not be used during pregnancy.

- Rose (*Rosa damascena*) is useful for soothing dry, irritated skin.

- Sweet orange (*Citrus sinensis*) is used as a digestive aid for constipation, flatulence and slow digestion, for relaxation, and as a nerve sedative. It is also great for colds, dull skin, flu, and for the gums and mouth.

- Tea tree essential oil (*Melaleuca alternifolia*), with its woodsy, earthy, herbaceous scent can treat thrush and is useful for cuts, scrapes, burns, and deep wound cleansing.

At two years old, the oils above as well as those below can be used:

- Clary sage (*Salvia sclarea*) is used for relaxation. Do not use during pregnancy.

- Eucalyptus (*Eucalyptus globulus*) can be used for the immune, respiratory, and skin systems of the body. It is cooling, stimulating, and penetrating and has strong antibacterial, antifungal, antiseptic, and antiviral compounds, so it is useful during the cold-weather season. It is sometimes used for skin conditions such as burns, ulcers, and wounds. Camphor-like, it is a common household remedy used in Australia to use the leaves and the oil for respiratory ailments such as bronchitis, croup, and fever caused by malaria, typhoid, cholera, etc. It also encourages emotional balance. It may help relieve the itch from chicken pox, but is for external use only. Not for use during pregnancy or by asthmatics.

- Ginger (*Zingiber officinale*) is helpful for nausea and diarrhea.

- Lemon oil (*Citrus limon)* helps the body face physical and psychological fatigue, most strongly influencing the mind by supporting concentration and the ability to memorize. In Japan, a test showed a 54 percent decrease in typing mistakes when lemon oil was diffused into an office area. Lemon is a natural antibacterial and antiviral, attributed to its limonene content which is why you will see it used to clean wooden butcher's blocks. People add lemon to their water to disinfect and to add valuable vitamins. Lemon is a first aid remedy as an astringent for the sting and itch of insect bites. Due to immune stimulating properties, Lemon Essential Oil should not be used topically on people who have an autoimmune disease. As with any citrus oil, do not use on skin when exposed to direct sunlight or apply it later, or from a tanning bed. Lemon, peppermint, and rosemary can be combined (after two years of age) into a carrier oil as a natural aid for constipation, when used with the colic-relief routine on the abdomen and foot through reflexology in Chapter Five.

- Peppermint *(Mentha piperita)* with a stronger mint scent than spearmint is used as a digestive aid, for headaches, nausea, fevers, cold and as a sedative. Do not use during pregnancy.

- Rosemary (*Rosmarinus officinalis)* is a great decongestant. It is good for asthma, bronchitis, whooping cough, colitis, dyspepsia, flatulence, dysmenorrhea, leucorrhea, colds, flu, infections, headaches, hypotension, neuralgia, mental fatigue, nervous exhaustion, and stress-related disorders. Rosemary is to be avoided during pregnancy and not to be used excessively by epileptics or those with high blood pressure.

- Tangerine *(Citrus reticulata)* is useful for lymphatic stimulation, upset stomach, and creating a calming atmosphere.

- <u>Calendula oil *(Calendula officinalis)* from the orange petals of the common marigold, is an anti-inflammatory that moisturizes and conditions baby's skin.</u>

Here is a list of essential oils that are not meant for aromatherapy use unless by a qualified aromatherapy practitioner, if at all (do not use on your baby): arnica, armoise, baldo leaf, bitter almond, calamus, horseradish, jaborandi leaf, mustard, pennyroyal, rue, sassafras, savin, souternwood, tansy, thuga, wormwood, and wintergreen.

For the massage oil, any pure cold-pressed vegetable, nut, seed, or fruit oil that is pesticide-free may be used as a massage oil on your baby's skin. These oils are easily absorbed by the skin and provide additional benefits to your child during and after the massage. During the massage, the skin will absorb these oils along with any added essential oils; there will be no oily residue you will have to wash off afterwards. I do not recommend olive oil for infant massage because its texture is too thick and it cannot be absorbed sufficiently by the skin.

Organic Jojoba Baby Oil, "Little Local Celebrity Organic Baby Oil," can be purchased at my site: www.LittleLocalCelebrity.com. The baby oil, either unscented or infused with organic lavender or chamomile essential oil, can be used on babies over three month old. We also sell "unscented," which can be used on babies and children of all ages.

Little known fact: Baby oil does not "cure" cradle cap. "All it does is hide the scales," says pediatrician Gary A. Emmett M.D., author of *Field Guide to the Normal Newborn.* Oil only softens the flakes so they become easy to brush off but does not stop them from forming again. Instead, he says, wash the baby's scalp with baby shampoo and rinse. Then apply a selenium-based dandruff shampoo and leave it on for five minutes. Rinse again, dry, and brush away the flakes. Always consult with your pediatrician prior to any home remedies.

What Type of Pressure Should I Apply to My Infant During the Massage?

During a study assessing the effects of moderate and light pressure massage on the growth and development of young infants, it was found that infants in the moderate-pressure massage group were more alert while the infants in the light-pressure massage group were more excitable, agitated, and fussy. The moderate-pressure infants exhibited greater weight gain and a greater increase in body length.

The same effects can be seen in adults receiving massage. In a study, three types of commonly used massage therapy techniques were assessed: (1) moderate massage pressure, (2) light massage pressure, or (3) vibratory stimulation group. Changes in anxiety and stress were assessed, and EEG and EKG were recorded. Anxiety scores decreased for all groups, but the moderate pressure massage group reported the greatest decrease in stress.

The moderate massage group also experienced a decrease in heart rate and EEG changes including an increase in delta and a decrease in alpha and beta activity, suggesting a relaxation response. Finally, this group showed increased positive affect, as indicated by a shift toward left frontal EEG activation. The light massage group showed increased arousal, as indicated by decreased delta and increased beta activity and increased heart rate. The vibratory stimulation group also showed increased arousal, as indicated by increased heart rate and increased theta, alpha, and beta activity.

We can conclude from this research that the best pressure to use in infants as well as adults is moderate pressure. Before you practice on your infant, find an adult and take their right hand in your left and glide up their arm from wrist to elbow with your thumb touching your fingertips, wrapped around like a circle around the wrist, "milking" their forearm. Try different pressures, begin with light and increase to a moderate that feels good to them. You will want to try the same pressure test on your infant. When you begin the massage strokes on the foot and leg, begin with light strokes and increase pressure to moderate when you are comfortable and note your baby's delight!

Chapter Five: Introducing Your Touch to Baby—Making First Contact: Foot and Leg Reflexology Infant Massage Routine

Before you begin any infant massage or touch routine, it is important to decompress from the stress in your daily life. This can be achieved through guided relaxation—and older children can participate as well.

Guided Relaxation

If you will be doing this alone, it's best to either purchase a guided relaxation CD or read the section below slowly into a recorder; when you need it you will have a copy and all you'll need to do is press play for instant relaxation. You can also have someone read this aloud to you.

To begin, lie down on your back on the floor, let yourself wiggle around until you are comfortable with palms facing up. Take a moment to breathe in deeply, focusing on filling your rib cage and belly with air. With exhalation, make a noise to dispel any stress you have been storing. Repeat this until you feel your stress has been dispelled. With your eyes closed, focus your breathing on creating stillness within. Allow your feet to relax and fall apart.

Feel your right hand; it is heavy and relaxed. Relax your thumb, pointer finger, middle finger, ring finger, pinky, your palm and the back of your hand. Taking a deep breath in, focus on relaxing your hand as you breathe out. ("Night-night hand" may be incorporated for youngsters.)

Feel your right arm; it is heavy and relaxed. Relax your wrist, lower arm, elbow, upper arm and your shoulder. Taking a deep breath in, exhale focusing on your right arm. ("Night-night right arm")

Repeat, replacing the right hand/arm and body parts with left hand, left arm and shoulder. Continue with your right foot, right leg and buttock, left foot, left leg and buttock, neck, head, chest, and belly.

To end, rename each body part you relaxed and feel it heavy and relaxed. Now you are ready to begin to share your feeling of relaxation with your child.

Still Touch and Kangaroo Care

Still Touch and Kangaroo Care are techniques that are wonderful to introduce touch to your child. They benefit well babies as well as those with special needs and those born prematurely, or in the NICU.

Still Touch

To begin touch with your infant, use Still Touch by simply cupping your hands around your child's feet, legs, body, arms, and head—each individually for a few moments before switching to the next part. The routine is as follows:

For the first hold, cup your hands underneath the baby's back and hold to allow the baby to get used to your touch. Relax and try to communicate love with each hold for a few minutes before moving on. For the second hold, you will cup your hand on your child's feet and legs and be still while softly holding them for a few minutes. The third hold will be with your infant's arms—softly cup them and practice a still hold for a few minutes. Release and move onto cupping their chest and abdomen and use a still hold for a few minutes. End with cupping your hands softly on the top of your baby's head and bottom, and hold for a few minutes.

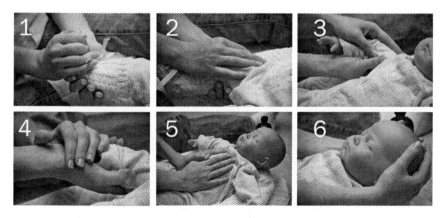

The Kangaroo Hold

Kangaroo Care originated in the 1980's in Columbia when two neonatologists observed that when infants received this form of touch in the NICU, the rate of mortality among premature babies fell from 70 to 30 percent. Kangaroo Care, also known as skin-to-skin care, is when the infant (bare except for a diaper and cap) is placed on the parents' bare chest, with the infant's head turned to the side so that the infants' ear is against the parent's chest, over their heart.

It has been proven to increase sleep time for babies of all ages. For preterm babies in particular, there is an average four-fold decrease in apnea (periods of not breathing,) the heart rate was more regular, the infants were eight times more likely to breastfeed spontaneously, and the mother and infant displayed thermal synchrony (if the baby's temperature lowered, the mother's would raise to warm the baby and vice versa) during Kangaroo Care.

For further information on Kangaroo Care benefits, please visit: www. geocities.com/roopage. Krisanne Collard is a leading expert on Kangaroo Care, and she personally saw benefits with her own premature infant, who weighed in at only 1 pound, 12 ounces at birth.

Some Infant Massage Precautions

Infants who are medically unstable, on ventilators, and who may have significant postoperative or post-procedural discomfort, should be handled as gently as possible. Smaller and less mature infants (less than 32 weeks post-conception age, and/or under 1200 grams) may not benefit from massage, and could potentially be at risk from this type of interaction. Other infants who are older, but who show similar disorganization, should not be provided with massage intervention.

Infants with chronic illness such as bronchopulmonary dysplasia and cardiac involvement have been shown to have physiologic and behavioral disorganization as well, and massage should be carefully weighed against the potential risks. Please be sure to speak with the NICU staff on what is best for your infant. They may instruct you to do Still Touch with your infant, or to wait until your infant is ready for touch stimulation. Some babies are extremely sensitive and will become overstimulated with more than one stimulus (any modality of communication) happening at the same time. Be sure to separate infant massage with talking and singing if this happens, and build incorporation slowly.

Infant Massage Techniques for the Feet and Leg

Feet are a great area to introduce massage to your infant because it is an area where your infant will not guard and will naturally relax the rest of his or her body in response to the massaging of the feet. Before you begin any massage, please take a few moments to breathe deeply, relax and focus all your attention on this special time you are about to share with your little one.

Babies who are 0-3 months usually still hold their arms in tight, with clenched fists, and become anxious when their arms are massaged, but they enjoy having their legs and back massaged.

Apply oil and warm it in your hands by rubbing them together, as needed, before beginning. This will avoid a feeling of friction on baby's skin as well as ensuring a warm application your baby will enjoy.

Gliding

Holding your baby's foot in the opposite hand from the leg you are working on, wrap your right hand around the baby's left ankle. With your left hand, glide from ankle to the top of the leg and wrap around the top of the thigh and glide back down to the ankle, in a continuous movement. Repeat a few times.

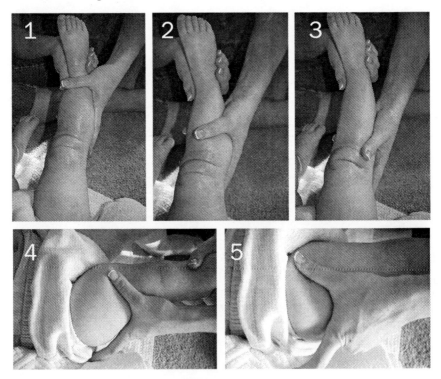

Next, glide from ankle to knee and back down and repeat.

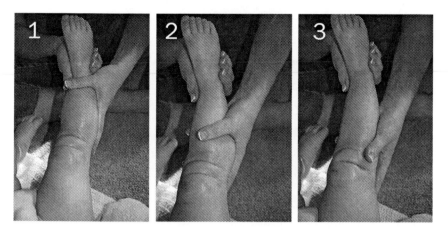

After you have done this stroke a few times, glide from the knee up to the top of the leg, around the buttocks, and around and back down again. Finish the leg by applying a few full-leg glides from ankle to top of thigh as shown or try to glide from the hip, around to the outer-side of the buttocks and back down and closing by holding baby's foot.

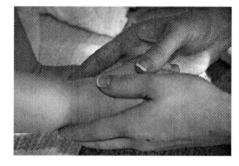

Repeat on the opposite leg by holding the baby's right ankle with your left hand and using your right hand to apply the strokes.

When first learning how to massage your infant's feet, you may want to follow the order outlined in this manual; however, you may find your baby enjoys some strokes more than others, and you can spend more or less time with those strokes and in any order you enjoy, later on when you are more comfortable with them.

In Reflexology, the toes are connected to the organs in the uppermost part of the body. The toes reflex and affect many areas. Focus on comforting the reflexing areas that correspond to the bottom of the foot as indicated below: heel: pelvic area, mid-section parallel to arch: internal organs, and the pads beneath the toes: chest/lung area.

When you are ready, apply a dime-sized amount of oil, lotion, or cream to your own hands and warm your hands by rubbing them together. Repeat this procedure any time you start to feel friction throughout the massage.

Still Touch

Next, place your hands around your baby's foot. It may be comfortable with one hand placed on top of the baby's foot and the other on the sole or bottom of the foot.

Close your eyes and focus on communicating love and comfort; hold them there in a still touch, not moving them and with a firm pressure, and ask your baby if he or she is ready for a massage.

Wait a second, then begin to massage the feet as described below, one at a time. If this is not your first massage, you will recognize by your baby's non-verbal cues whether he or she wants a massage, or may rather be held or fed, etc. Try again later, perhaps after a bath or before bed. Please remember, each time you will begin on the left or right foot and leg and do all the strokes on that individual foot, ankle, and leg, before moving on to the opposite foot, ankle, and leg.

Sliding

Photo #1: From the holding position, slide both hands where your fingers are on top and towards the ankle with thumbs on the bottom, slide fingers towards the ankles. Pause for a second at the ankle with your bottom hand at the heel while the top hand makes a continuous movement over and around the outside ankle (#2 below).

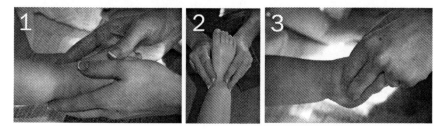

Photo #2: For another position with this stroke, you can position your right hand on top for the right ankle and your left hand on top for the left ankle in order to do a smooth continuous circle around the ankle with your outside hand.

Photo #3: To finish this stroke, rest your thumbs on top of the baby's foot and circle the anklebones on both sides with your fingertips.

Circles

Holding your baby's right foot in your left hand, use the pad of your thumb on your right hand to make circles in a clockwise motion.

 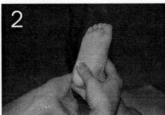 

Spreading

 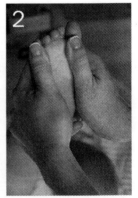

Glide your thumbs to the bottom of the foot side by side, with your thumbs pressing lightly up and into the sole of the foot. Spread the foot by pressing down toward the sides of the foot using the fleshy pad at the base of your thumbs and upward from mid-sole to the outsides with your fingertips from the bottom. If you have nails, be careful to angle your fingertips so that only the pads of your fingers are pressing against your baby's foot. Repeat several times.

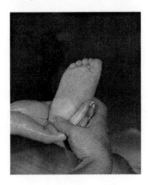

Gliding up Sole

Using your thumb, apply steady pressure at the heel, through the arch, and up until the base of the toes.

Reflexology for the Sole for Colic Relief:

Researchers have come a long way in determining the major cause of colic. The common conclusion is that colic is caused by a baby's (whether premature or full term) inability to transition from one sleep state to another; from an alert state into a sleep state and back again. The gas associated with colic is caused by the excess crying during these transitions. A routine to relieve this gas can be applied through reflexology to the feet and directly to the gastrointestinal tract.

Using your palm, glide up the left side of your baby's sole from above the heel line to right above the pads of the toes and go across to the right side and back down to the heel line and over. This stroke stimulates diastalsis (movement in the abdominal organs) and corresponds to the organs in the gastrointestinal tract providing relief to colic and other tummy-related problems.

As you are gliding up the left side, focus on the reflexing movement of your baby's ascending colon. While gliding across the pads below the toes, focus on stimulating movement of the transverse colon. Gliding down the right side of your baby's sole, focus on the descending colon. While coming across the heel line, focus on the sigmoid colon and relieving your baby's gastrointestinal distress.

Step 1:

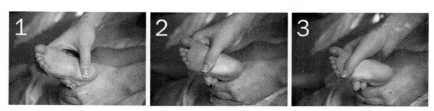

Step 2:

Step 3:

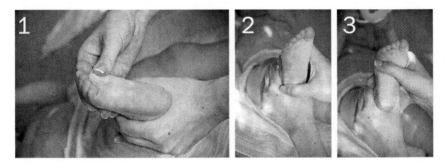

Rolling

Place hands on either side of your baby's heel, so that your fingertips are facing away from you and make quick back-and-forth movements, where your hands go in opposite directions. This should roll baby's foot back and forth repeatedly from left to right.

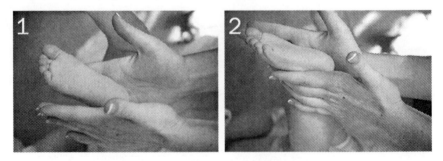

Milking

Grasp your baby's foot with your thumbs on the bottom, one above another, and your fingers across the top, and squeeze from the ankle to the tip of the toes and glide back down to the ankle with your hands in a looser position; repeat.

Gliding and Toe Pulls

Supporting the foot on one side, glide your thumb between the bones of the foot, from the toes to the ankle. Maintaining contact the entire time, use more pressure in your glide towards the ankle and less in the return stroke to help aid in circulation. You can also end each stroke with a gentle toe pull.

Toe Pulls: Hold your baby's foot in one hand. Using your thumb and forefinger, gently pull and twist, gliding off each toe with either a straight off-pull or a side-to-side motion. You can incorporate "This little piggy" Nursery rhyme lyrics that follow.

This Little Piggy Nursery Rhyme Song

Action: Each little piggy line correlates to a toe, starting with the big toe you slowly wiggle each one while singing then with the last line you increase the wiggling and tickle the littlest toe and foot.

Song: This little piggy went to market,
   this little piggy stayed at home,
   this little piggy had roast beef,
   and this little piggy had none.
   And this little piggy went
   "Wee wee wee," all the way home... [36]

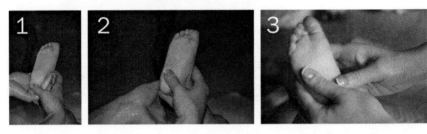

Circles

Place both hands on your baby's foot with your fingertips on the top of the foot and your thumbs on the sole/bottom of his/her foot. Begin making small circles on the bottom of the foot with the pads of your thumbs, from heel up through the sole to the pads underneath the toes.

Next, you can use a thumb-over-thumb glide to cover the entire bottom of the foot from the heel to the toes photographed on following page.

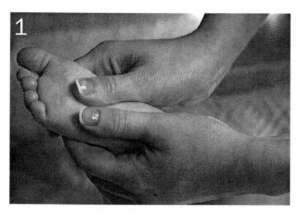
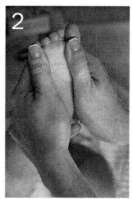

To end the session with the foot and signify to your baby that you are ready to move onto the leg, lightly brush the foot with your fingertips from the ankle to the toes, and then use a still-hold with both hands for a few seconds and release. You can also accompany this still touch with telling your child, "Now we're going to massage your legs!"

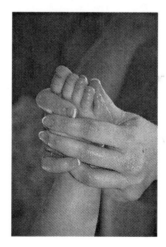

Chapter Six: Infant Massage Techniques for the Hand and Arm

Reapply warm oil in hands, as needed. Begin by holding your baby's hand supportively, taking a moment to notice what your baby's hand feels like in size, temperature, strength, and weight. Apply the oil to your hands and warm, applying extra oil, if required.

Hand Spreading

With your thumbs side-by-side on top, press down gently on your baby's hand at the same time that your fingertips press up underneath. Then spread the hand slowly from the center out by rotating your thumbs in towards each other and pulling up with your fingers; repeat several times.

Glide

Support your baby's hand on one side and, using your thumb and forefinger, glide up from the base of the knuckles to the wrist. Finish with small circles on top of and under the wrist.

Finger Pulls

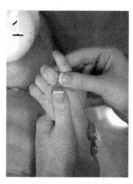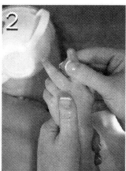

Next, massage the fingers. Holding your babies wrist with one hand, grab a finger with your thumb and forefinger and pull from the base of the finger until you glide off the tip. You can pull straight off or add a twist from side to side for variety. Massage each finger. You may want to incorporate the "Where is Thumbkin?" nursery rhyme.

Where is Thumbkin? Nursery Rhyme song:

Actions: Hold up one thumb, then the other, then motion thumbs so it looks like they are talking to each other. Then one at a time, put your hands behind your back. Move onto pointer, middle, ring, and pinky fingers.

"Where is thumbkin? Where is thumbkin? Here I am.
Here I am.
How are you today sir? Very well I thank you. Run away.
Run away.
Where is pointer? Where is pointer? Here I am. Here I
am.
How are you today sir? Very well I thank you. Run away.
Run away.
Where is middle finger? Where is middle finger? Here I

am. Here I am.
How are you today sir? Very well I thank you. Run away.
Run away.
Where is ring finger? Where is ring finger? Here I am.
Here I am.
How are you today sir? Very well I thank you. Run away.
Run away.
Where is pinky? Where is pinky? Here I am. Here I am.
How are you today sir? Very well I thank you. Run away.
Run away."

Pat-a-Cake Nursery Rhyme song:

Pat-a-cake, pat-a-cake,
Baker's man!
Bake us a cake
as fast as you can,
(Action: Alternate clapping baby's hands and yours)
Mix it and prick it
(Action: Pretend to stir bowl, then prick cake)
and mark it with B*,
(Action: Make a 'B*' in the air)
and there will be plenty
for baby* and me.
(Action: Alternate clapping baby's hands and yours)

*Note: To make it more personal you can also use the first letter of your child's name, for instance: "...and mark it with a C, and there will be plenty for Chloe and me." You can also sing this song over again, to incorporate all of your children's names.

ONE, TWO, THREE Nursery Rhyme song: Count on Baby's Fingers:

One, two, three, four, five,
once I caught a fish alive.
Six, seven, eight, nine, ten,

but I let it go again.
Why did you let it go?
Because it bit my finger so.
Which finger did it bite?
This little one upon the right.

Palm Spreading

With the palm facing you and your thumbs positioned on the babies palm and fingertips on the top of their hand, press down gently and spread to the outside of the palm with the pads of your thumb. You can also leave your thumbs in place and press down gently while spreading your fingertips to the outsides of the top of the hand.

Arm:

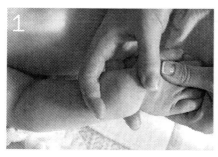 

Gliding and Kneading the Forearm

With your hand positioned in a C shape, use a gentle stroke to glide from the wrist to the elbow and back. Try applying more pressure on the stroke towards the elbow and less on the return stroke. Practice on both sides of the forearm. Then, on the top of the forearm practice applying a small circular stroke using your thumbs with your fingertips positioned on the bottom of the forearm for support.

Nerve Stroke

Continue the glide from the wrist to the shoulder. After repeating the stroke a few times, spread the palm of the hand once again as you did in the beginning and finish the hand and arm with a light brushing nerve stroke by lightly brushing the arm from shoulder to the tips of the fingers with your fingertips. Another additional comforting finish is to simply hold your baby's hand after this last stroke and then gently release.

Repeat with opposite hand and arm before moving on to the next area.

Chapter Seven: Infant Massage Routine for the Chest and Abdomen

Chest Spread

Place your hands with your palms together and thumbs up. Apply them to your baby's chest and spread pinkies first, to your baby's sides and glide around the sides, and back around until your palms are together again. Repeat several times.

Shoulder Glides

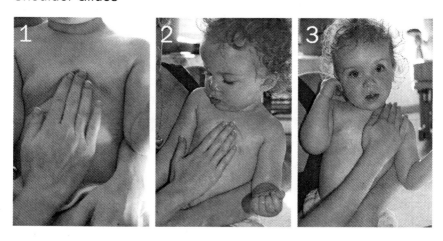

Using the opposite hand from the shoulder you are approaching, start at the baby's chest and wrap around the back of the shoulder with a very gentle downward pull to stretch the muscles of the shoulder.

Then glide back and off the ribs on the opposite side. Repeat and then practice on the other side.

Chest Stretch

With your baby lying on his or her back in front of you, have them hold onto your thumbs and grasp their little hands and outstretch their arms to the sides. Then bring the arms across the chest, gently crossing them.

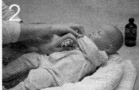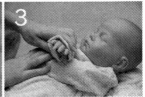

Opposite Arm to Leg Stretch (Photos #1 & 2 below)

Parent's right hand holds baby's left hand and parent's left hand holds baby's right foot. Bring arm down and leg up until they meet mid-air, gently. Then repeat, this time trying to reach the toe and hand to the baby's nose. Do not force the stretch to literally touch the nose. Repeat, then switch sides.

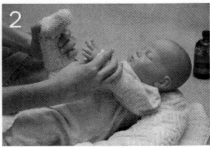

Colic-Relief Sequence For The Abdomen For this abdomen techniques, all strokes will follow a clockwise pattern (to the right, around in a circle.) It is important the strokes go this direction to follow your baby's natural underlying gastrointestinal tract movement and thus, stimulate movement.

Colic-Relief Sequence for the Abdomen

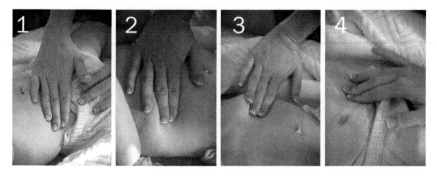

Using your palm, glide up the left side of your baby's abdomen from above the pelvic line to right above the waist line and go across to the right side and back down to the pelvic line and over. This stroke stimulates diastalsis (movement in the abdominal organs) and corresponds to the organs in the gastrointestinal tract providing relief to colic and other tummy-related problems.

As you are gliding up the left side, focus on the reflexing movement of your baby's ascending colon. While gliding across the waist line, focus on stimulating movement of the transverse colon. Gliding down the right side of your baby's abdomen, focus on the descending colon. While coming across the pelvic line, focus on the sigmoid colon and relieving your baby's gastrointestinal distress.

You can also attempt this stroke with both hands, using your right thumb or palm (depending on your infant's size) for gliding up the left side and over the waistline and then your left hand going down the right and over the pelvic line, with a hand-over-hand technique, often referred to as the sun and the moon.

Holding one leg by the shin in each hand, gently move the legs back and forth in a pedaling fashion. Repeat a few times.

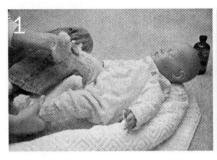 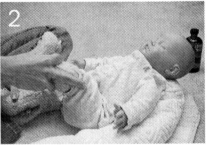

Holding one leg by the shin in each hand, gently move the legs in one fluid motion, toward the belly, hold and release. Baby's legs should bend at the knees.

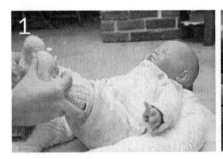 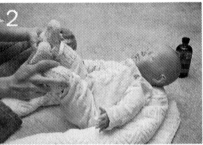

Place your hand right below your infant's rib cage, palm down, and slide down to the pelvic line and repeat with opposite hand in a rhythmic fashion.

Head, Shoulders, Knees and Toes song
Lyrics to the tune "London Bridge":

> Head and shoulders, knees and toes,
>> Knees and toes,
>> Knees and toes,
>> Head and shoulders, knees and toes,
>> It's my body!
>
> Eyes and ears and mouth and nose,
> Mouth and nose,
> Mouth and nose,
> Eyes and ears and mouth and nose,
> It's my body!

Ankles, elbows, feet and seat,
Feet and seat,
Feet and seat,
Ankles, elbows, feet and seat,
It's my body!

This song can be sung while touching the various "It's my body" parts and is sure to amuse your young one!

Chapter Eight: Different Holding Positions and Infant Massage Routine for Baby's Back

To begin massaging your baby's back, you can position her stomach towards you over your shoulder, across your lap on her belly or in your arm in a "football hold," stomach down.

Back Glide

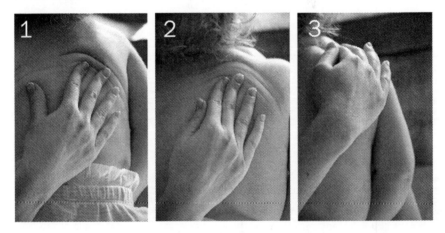

With one of your hands palm down (or both if they fit alongside each side of the spine), right above your baby's buttocks, glide up through the top of the neck and come together with your fingertips in the middle. Next, glide out to the sides and back down and repeat.

Back/Shoulder Glide

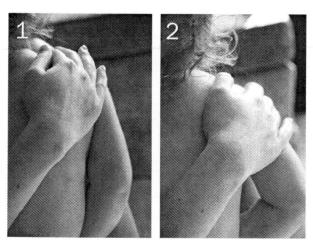

Repeat the same stroke, but this time, when you approach the neck, sway to the side and glide over the shoulder (providing a light downward stretch for the shoulder) and then glide back down. Repeat this stroke a few times for both shoulders.

Neck

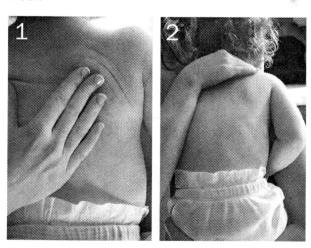

Glide up baby's back until you reach her neck. At the neck, wrap your hand gently around the side and back of the neck only and pull gently out towards the back, in a milking fashion; repeat several times.

Lower Back/Buttocks Circles

Using your palm or the pads and sides of your thumbs, massage the lower back and buttocks in circles, from the side of the hip toward the center. Maintaining enough distance so that you don't spread the buttocks with the massage. Then continue in your stroke up and around.

Chapter Nine: Infant Massage Routine for the Face

Gentle pressure is preferred in facial massage. No oil is needed for these strokes; however, an oil or lotion may be applied to your hands to reduce friction if desired. Please make sure it is safe to use on babies' faces in advance.

Forehead

From the eyebrows to the hairline, brush the forehead with your fingertips or thumbs in alternating strokes. Repeat.

Finish the forehead by aligning your palms together and spreading them from the center of the forehead out to the temples, pausing with each spread at the temples and doing small circles there. Make small circles on the temples.

Eyebrows: Stroke from the middle to the temples, with light pressure on top of the eyebrows. Make small circles at the temples.

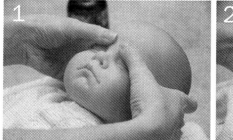

Eyelids: If your baby will rest his or her eyelids, gently press from the center out to the temples, finishing with circles on top of the temples.

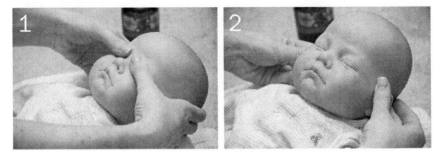

Nose and Cheeks

Starting at the top of the nose, stroke down the sides of the base of the nose. Using your fingertips, follow your baby's cheek bone to the ears, either making small circles or applying gentle, continuous pressure. Make small circles on the temples when you end each stroke.

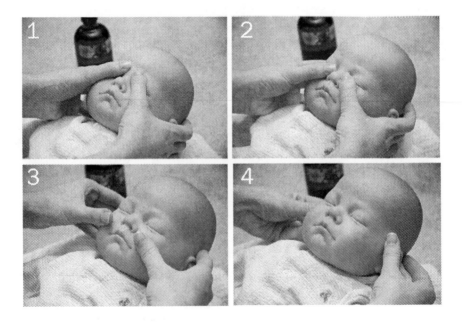

Upper Lip and Chin

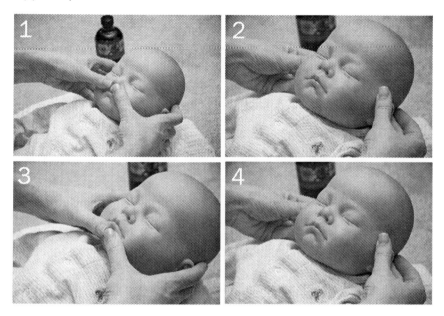

With your thumbs centered on the baby's upper lip, stroke out towards the temples finishing with circles. After a few strokes, center your thumbs below the bottom lip and circle up towards the temples, finishing with circles on top of the temples.

Circles on Ears

Starting at the top of the ear make small circles on the ear until you reach the bottom and glide off. 'Do your ears hang low?' is a great sing-along song to do with this massage stroke.

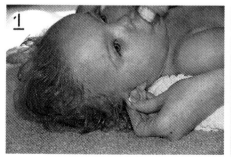
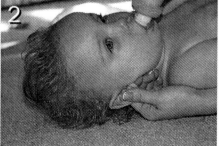

Song: Do Your Ears Hang Low?

> Do your ears hang low?
>> Do they wobble to and fro?
>> Can you tie them in a knot?
>> Can you tie them in a bow?
>> Do your ears hang low?

Scalp Circles

With your baby's head cradled in your hands and your fingertips under his or her head, do small circles with your fingertips. Continue massaging the entire scalp. You can also use an in and out movement with your fingers as if you were shampooing his or her hair to cover the head. A lot of tension resides in this area, so be sure to cover the sides of the scalp as well by gently turning the head.

Chapter Ten: Ending Your Infant Massage and Post-Partum Tandem Exercise Routine for Mother and Baby

After you have completed the infant massage routine with your child, swaddle baby in a blanket, as infant massage increases circulation and tends to make the air feel cooler to your baby.

Specific activities, exercises, and stretches can be utilized that help strengthen muscles and promote babies' natural growth through stages in communication, physical activities, and interpersonal/social skills from the very beginning. As your baby starts to develop certain skills, you are able to play an important role in assisting your baby's development.

Babies are capable of understanding and learning any language very easily, more so before age 10 months. If you are interested in helping your baby develop skills in another language, the earlier the better. Remember, all babies develop at a different pace—it doesn't make one smarter or better than another. Let your baby set the pace for exploring his or her new world.

The activities listed are made for at home use for parents with the children. There are several companies embracing this concept. For example, Gymboree—a company made to assist parents in planned activities specific for each stage of development, while also providing time for personal play and group songs and activities—is one I personally used with my daughter and thoroughly enjoyed. The classes would always give me ideas to push her to try new things. I wasn't aware she could do because we just never tried.

Considering that she was my first child, these activities helped me let her go and explore in a safe environment, which (as any first-time mom knows) can be hard to do. It also helped her increase sociability, surrounding her with children of the same age who become familiar in time and may turn out to be your child's first friends. The classes also provide first experiences with the opportunity to interact with other babies their age. It is just as valuable if it is a second or sixth child, as it will give you one-on-one time with just that individual child, perhaps while the older children are in school.

Training Pre-, During and Postpartum

In a society where fitness, health and beauty is all the rage, we are going beyond aesthetics to discover a wealth of practical and long term physical benefits to strength and cardiovascular training, particularly concerning pre and postpartum pregnancy. According to an article on BJSM on line, quoting new guidelines of The American College of Obstetricians and Gynecologists for exercise in pregnancy and postpartum, http://bjsportmed.com/cgi/content/extract/37/1/6:

> "Pregnancy is recognized–as a unique time for behavior modification and is no longer–considered a condition for confinement. It is currently recognized–that habits adopted during pregnancy could affect a woman's–health for the rest of her life. The recommendations also promote exercise for sedentary women–and those with medical or obstetric complications, but only after medical evaluation and clearance. There are no published–studies to indicate that, in the absence medical complications, rapid resumption of activities will result in adverse effects."

With this in mind, it is still important to clear all recommencement of exercise during and postpartum with your physician.

Depending upon current fitness levels, women can usually safely and effectively start and continue with an exercise program at any time during and after pregnancy. Strength and cardiovascular conditioning are extremely important to help women make it through the nine months of stress pregnancy induces on the body. Not to mention, the importance of being in "good shape" for labor and recovery. We train to run marathons, why shouldn't we train for the "marathon" of labor.

If you're not familiar with exercising in a gym, it is a great idea to hire a trainer. They are able to make sure you are doing the proper exercises with proper form. Not only is it important for you as a pregnant woman to have good form while performing exercises, at some point everyone working out solo should have some expert coaching at one time or another. Injuries can happen quickly with long-term repercussions, and it's just not worth it. You should always look for a trainer who is qualified to help you with your needs as an expectant or new mother. Always check for current certifications and qualifications. You can never be too careful with this, as different states have different laws and requirements for personal trainers. Some states don't require certifications!

Since everyone's healing time differs it is difficult to determine an exact benchmark for resuming exercise after delivery. The Guidelines from the American College of Obstetricians and Gynecologists (ACOG), say that after delivery women may resume exercise "as soon as it is medically safe." For some women this means days for others weeks or months. This depends largely on delivery circumstances (natural or cesarean). Although, it is wise to obtain clearance from your physician, it is also wise to use your discomfort level as a point of reference. In other words, if it hurts, don't do it. Wait several days and try again.

Most experts advise mothers to wait at least six weeks before beginning any form of rigorous exercise, but interestingly in an article from the Certified News by American Council on Exercise (ACE)

> "according to Davies, the lead author of the Society of Obstetricians and Gynecologists of Canada (SOGC) and the Canadian Society for Exercise Physiology (CSEP) , the medical teaching has probably been too conservative regarding post partum exercise for women who have had cesarean section. I don't see a problem for the majority of women whose pain is well-managed and feel they want to return to more activity sooner [than six weeks to do so]."

> Davies also says, "with respect to abdominal exercises, yoga with abdominal stretching and weight training, it is best for women to wait four to eight weeks post-operation, depending on their pre-delivery fitness level, their post-operative hemoglobin level and overall energy. The concern with significant abdominal exercise too soon after a cesarean section would be disruption of

the fascial repair and the development of a hernia," (Although, he adds, hernia rates are extremely low with the type of cesarean incision that is most common today.) Gentle movement such as walking may be appropriate for certain clients in the early weeks after delivery. Otherwise, the six-week timeline is a typical benchmark for resuming exercise." (Volume 13, Number 3, p. 8-9)

In my experience, the sooner you get moving the better and the faster the healing process will occur. Obviously, don't over do it, you just had major surgery and again, use that level of discomfort as your guide. If it hurts, stop!

Another issue that concerns women recovering from c-section, is the idea that their abdominal muscles were cut. This idea can sometimes be a subconscious debilitator, causing women to not knowingly inhibit themselves from using their abdominals. This non-usage creates a weakness and, in turn, slows their overall fitness progress. But the idea of cut abdominal muscles is, in most cases a fallacy. In fact, "The most common type of c-section is a transverse incision about an inch above the pubic bone. This procedure is how 90 percent of cesareans are performed, says Gregory Davies, M. D., of Kingston General Hospital in Kingston, Ontario. Here, he summarizes how it's done:

"the incision, which is called the Pfannenstiel incision, does not actually cut muscle. After incising the skin and subcutaneous fat, the fascia of the internal and external oblique muscles is incised, but not the muscles themselves. The rectus abdominis is then divided in the midline, and, again not cut. The peritoneum [membrane that lines the abdominal cavity] is then entered, and now one is inside the abdominal cavity."

Now concerning exercise modalities, it is best to pace yourself. Do not do too much too soon. When you doctor gives you the okay, I suggest starting with 2 to 3 strength training sessions a week accompanied by a few sessions of relatively intense cardio. A good suggestion might be to do your strength training sessions at a cardio pace to get the best of both worlds. Mix it up and get creative. It's important not to let the body adapt because it will eventually become efficient at performing a repetitive stimulus, therefore limiting improvement. So, keep the body guessing. Start with a 5-10 minute warm up, followed by 20-30 minutes of free-weight and or body weight bearing exercises. Perform, initially, 6-10 repetitions of each exercise. These exercises need not be complex. They can be as simple as body weight squats. You may want to do more than 6-10 reps. of these as they probably won't be very challenging with just your body weight. For goodness sake, you just carried a baby around in your belly for nine months. Let's make it a little bit challenging), followed by a dumbbell row or lat pull down, and push-ups. No bicep curls please! Bicep curls are a single joint movement that uses very little energy and does little to improve overall fitness. We're trying to raise our heart rate, burn fat, and get strong. By doing compound, multi-joint exercises you are using your time wisely and utilizing your energy more efficiently, therefore burning more calories and helping reach your goal more successfully. For example: when doing a pushup the majority of the eccentric work is done by the chest and triceps muscles, but the back, abdominal and majority of the trunk musculature is used for stabilization. Now that sounds more efficient than a silly little bicep curl! As far as abdominal training goes, initially, modifications or avoidance altogether may be necessary, and pelvic floor exercises are a must! (aka kegles. We know what those are, don't we girls?) A qualified personal trainer will be able to enrich and expand upon all of the above information. Good Luck!

Excerpt on Training Pre-, During and Postpartum, by Christy Nielsen co-owner of CrossFit Alexandria, Personal Trainer, AFAA and CrossFit certified. www.CrossFitAlexandria.com

You may email Christy at: CrossFitAlexandria@hotmail.com

Works cited

http://bjsportmed.com/cgi/content/extract/37/1/6

2. ACE Certified News. Volume 13. Number3. p. 8-9.

Post-partum Exercises for Mother with the Baby in Tow!

Please be sure to discuss this program with your doctor before beginning. Never release your grasp of the baby while exercising and lifting baby off the floor. If exercising with the baby starts to compromise your form or posture, consider trying the exercises below by yourself or with weights that are lighter than the baby while he or she is sleeping.

There are a variety of nursery rhymes you can sing while you exercise, I provided a few below each exercise. One that usually gets me through a few different exercises is, "London Bridge Is Falling Down."

London Bridge Is Falling Down

London Bridge is falling down,
Falling down, falling down,
London Bridge is falling down,
My fair Lady.

Build it up with wood and clay,
Wood and clay, wood and clay,
Build it up with wood and clay,
My fair Lady.

Wood and clay will wash away,
Wash away, wash away,
Wood and clay will wash away,
My fair Lady.

Build it up with bricks and mortar,
Bricks and mortar, bricks and mortar,
Build it up with bricks and mortar,
My fair Lady.

Bricks and mortar will not stay,
Will not stay, will not stay,
Bricks and mortar will not stay,
My fair Lady.

Build it up with iron and steel,
Iron and steel, iron and steel,
Build it up with iron and steel,
My fair Lady.

Iron and steel will bend and bow,
Bend and bow, bend and bow,
Iron and steel will bend and bow,
My fair Lady.

Build it up with silver and gold,
Silver and gold, silver and gold,
Build it up with silver and gold,
My fair Lady.

Silver and gold will be stolen away,
Stolen away, stolen away,
Silver and gold will be stolen away,
My fair Lady.

Set a man to watch all nigh,
Watch all night, watch all night,
Set a man to watch all night,
My fair Lady.

Suppose the man should fall asleep,
Fall asleep, fall asleep,
Suppose the man should fall asleep?
My fair Lady.

Give him a pipe to smoke all night,
Smoke all night, smoke all night,
Give him a pipe to smoke all night,
My fair Lady.

Peek-a-boo Tilt/Sit-ups

In a seated position, with your knees bent, lay baby on your thighs, seated into your belly. Hold onto your baby either by his hands or body and lean back as far as possible and hold for as long as you can. If this is too hard, begin with regular crunch sit-ups in this position with the baby.

Little Local Celebrity Leg Lifts

Lie on your back with knees at a 90-degree angle and baby resting atop your shins. Lower your legs, with the angle between your heels and buttocks decreasing, then lift back to the starting position. Keep your lower back pressed against the floor throughout the entire movement.

To increase the level of this exercise, lift in thirds: the first time, lift only a third of the way up, the second time two-thirds of the way, and the third time all the way up. Do as many reps as you can, or baby lets you!

"Jack be nimble, Jack be quick, Jack jump over (lift legs!), the candlestick!"

"Hickory dickory dock
The mouse ran up the clock (raise legs.)
The clock struck one, (lower legs)

"Cuckoo" (raise legs!)
The mouse ran down (lower legs!)
Hickory dickory dock."

Airplane Blastoff

Lie on your back and bend your knees into your chest, placing your baby on top of your shins, with his head peeking over at you. Get a firm grasp of your baby and move your legs up and down and in circles, to the side and all around, pretending your baby is a plane! Be careful to always make sure to have a good grip on your child!

You can sing "Ring around the rosies, Pocket full of posies, Ashes, ashes, We all fall down!" which you can incorporate into your movements!

Sugar and Spice Crunches

From the Airplane Blastoff position, bring your knees into your chest while you crunch up and tighten your abdominal or core muscles and kiss the baby! The further you can extend your legs with a good grip on your baby, the harder the exercise becomes!

Marching Bridge

With baby sitting atop your tummy, holding her firmly, lift your pelvis up and hold for a few seconds and release. Repeat. You can incorporate a song such as, "Jack and Jill went up the hill to fetch a pail of water, Jack fell down and broke his crown, And Jill came tumbling after. Up Jack got, and home did trot, As fast as he could caper, He went to bed and bound his head, with vinegar and brown paper."

Hop-on-Mom!

Lying down, grip your baby around his or her body (baby must be able to support his or her own head.) Bench press the baby. Bring down until your elbows are at a 90-degree angle, then lift extending your arms until right before they lock and repeat. "Here's the church, and here's the steeple, Open the door and see all the people, Here's the parson going upstairs, And here he is saying his prayers."

Smoochy Push-Up

Lay the baby underneath, while you do a push-up. Mommy kisses the baby each time as she lowers down onto the floor. You can lie on your knees to assist you doing a pushup. "What are little boys made of?

Snips and snails, and puppy dog tails, that's what little boys are made of!" or "What are little girls made of? Sugar and spice and all things nice, that's what little girls are made of!"

Horsey Extensions

Sit on the edge of a chair with both knees bent and flat on the floor. Place the baby on one shin. Hold onto his hands or body (whichever is better to have a firm grip) and straighten the leg that the baby is on. You can increase the level by raising your leg in thirds, e.g., the first time only raising the baby one-third of the way up, the second time two-thirds, and so on. Repeat with opposite leg. You can also use both legs at once as pictured below:

Resource Guide for New and Expectant Parents

ADA and Disability Information: www.usdoj.gov/crt/ada/adahom1. htm

The Alliance for Transforming the Lives of Children: This organization is dedicated to the synergistic marshalling of resources and connections to support parents, caregivers, professionals, and policymakers in practicing the art and science of nurturing children. 1-888-574-7580 www.atlc.org

The American Academy of Family Physicians: 800-274-2237

The American Academy of Pediatrics: 847-434-4000; www.aap.org

The American Council for the Blind: 800-424-8666

The American Kidney Foundation: 800-622-9010

American Social Health Association: 800-230-6039

American Speech Language Association: www.asha.org

Attachment Parenting International (API): Advocates attachment parenting methods to develop and fulfill a child's need for trust, empathy, and affection to create secure relationships. 615-298-4334; www.attachmentparenting.org

Autism Society: www.autism.org

Baby Center Cradle and All: www.babycenter.com

Baby Wit Boutique: www.babywit.com/Merchant2/merchant. mvc?Screen=SFNT&Store_Code=BW&Affiliate=14029

CDC National AIDS Hotline: 800-342-2437

Centers for Medicare & Medicaid Services: 877-267-2323

Cerebral Palsy Information: www.ucp.org

Child Care Aware: www.childcareaware.org

Childhelp's National Child Abuse Hotline: 800-422-4453; Adult and Child Abuse Reporting: 800-752-6200

Children with Attention Deficit Disorder: www.chaddnline.org

Crib Death (SIDS) National Hotline: 800-221-7437

CPR Certification with the National Safety Council: 800-621-7619; www.nsc.org

Down Syndrome Information: www.ndss.org

Dr. Bronner's: www.drbronner.com Organic Baby Soap!

The Fatherhood Project: www.fatherhoodproject.com

Food and Nutrition Service (FNS), a Federal agency of the U.S. Department of Agriculture, responsible for administering the WIC Program: www.fns.usda.gov/wic; Washington DC residents 1-800-345-1942; Virginia 1-888-942-3663; Maryland 1-800-242-4942. Residents of other states, please call one of the 800 numbers listed and ask for your state agency contact information. WIC provides supplemental nutritious foods; nutrition education and counseling at WIC clinics; screening and referrals to other health, welfare, and social services to low-income, nutritionally at risk:

- Pregnant women (through pregnancy and up to 6 weeks after birth or after pregnancy ends)

- Breastfeeding women (up to infant's 1st birthday)

- Non-breastfeeding postpartum women (up to 6 months after the birth of an infant or after pregnancy ends)

- Infants (up to 1st birthday). WIC serves 45 percent of all infants born in the United States and children up to their 5th birthday

Foster Parent Homepage : www.fostercare.org

Gymboree Play and Music Classes: www.playandmusic.com/b2c/customer/home.jsp; 1-877-4-GYMWEB (1-877-449-6932) from Monday through Friday, 6:00 AM to 9:00 PM and Saturday, 7:00 AM to 3:00 PM, Pacific Time. Call to find a location to try a free play or music class today!

Healthy Steps for Young Children Program: www.healthysteps.org

Hip & Little! The Children's Boutique at Hip and Little specializes in cute baby things, hard to find gifts, and many handmade children's items: ww8.aitsafe.com/go.htm?go=www.hipandlittle.com&afid=14029&tm=&im=1

Homeschool Support Network: (www.homeeducator.com/HSN/information.htm)

I am your Child: www.iamyourchild.org

KidsSource Online: www.kidsource.com

Kindersign Baby Sign Language University: To sign up for a Baby Signing Workshop in the NOVA/MD/DC area please visit: www.littlelocalcelebrity.com . If you are outside of those areas, please visit www.kinderworkshops.com to locate a local Instructor.

Language Lizard: Learning Materials for Infants and Children in 40+ Languages! www.languagelizard.com/?Click=508

La Leche League International provides support and encouragement to breastfeeding mothers, as well as a wealth of information on the subject. Regular support meetings can lead to the development of friendships, as well as contacts for playgroups and babysitting co-ops: 800-La Leche (800-525-3243) 9:00 a.m.–5:00 p.m., Monday–Friday (Central time)

Little Local Celebrity: Infant Massage, Baby Signing (Toddler and Preschool classes too!), Mommy and Baby Fitness Workshops, "Little Local Celebrity," Organic Jojoba Massage Oil, Boutique Items and more! 571-748-3855; www.littlelocalcelebrity.com

Mocha Moms Online is a site for stay at home mothers of color. Mocha Moms is a support group for stay at home mothers of color who have chosen not to work full-time outside of the home in order to devote more time to their families. www.mochamoms.org

MOMS Clubs are local support groups that meet during the day, are non-sectarian, and welcome all at-home mothers and their children. They offer speakers and discussion topics, family parties, playgroups, baby-sitting co-ops, special activity groups, community service projects, and more. For information about MOMS Clubs in your area or for help in starting a group, send $2.00 to: International MOMS Club, 464 Madera Rd., #N 191, Simi Valley, CA 93065.

MOPS (Mothers of Preschoolers) provide fellowship of mothers with young children, offering a nurturing, caring environment with a spiritual focus. Meetings follow the school calendar. Moms share information, have small group discussion time, and learn a craft, while children play nearby with supervision. 800-929-1287

Mothering Magazine is a magazine that celebrates the experience of parenthood as worthy of one's best efforts and fosters awareness of the immense importance and value of parenthood and family life in the development of the full human potential. www.LittleLocalCelebrity. com to place your subscription today or call 571-748-3855.

Mothers & More is a national support and advocacy group for women who have altered their career paths in order to care for their children at home. Local chapters sponsor regular meetings, playgroups, babysitting co-ops, and more. (630)941-3553 www.mothersandmore.org

Nationall Association of Child Care Resources and Referral Agencies: www.naccrra.net

National Association of Mother's Centers (NAMC) is a non-profit umbrella organization which includes 50 Mother's Centers across the country. Local centers sponsor workshops, seminars, groups, and special events and serve as a place where mothers can come together with other mothers and members of the professional community to explore the experience of becoming and being mothers. 516-520-2929 and 800-645-3828 www.motherscenter.org

National Capital Poison Control Hotline: 1-800-222-1222. Take steps to prevent poisoning! Store medicines and household products in their original containers. Lock medicines and household products where children cannot see or reach them. Use child-resistant packaging. Replace the caps tightly after using a product. Read the label before taking or giving medicine—every time. Use household products according to label directions. Mixing household products can cause dangerous gases to form. Install a carbon monoxide alarm. Store the number on your cell phone, memory on the home phone and in your phone book and have a friend do the same.

National Center for Fathering (www.fathers.com) is a non-profit organization who's mission is to inspire and prepare men to be better fathers. Founded in 1990 by Dr. Ken Canfield to conduct research on fathering and to develop practical resources for dads in nearly every fathering situation. If you'd like to contact then just send an e-mail to: dads@fathers.com, or call us at: 800-593-DADS.

National Domestic Violence Hotline 800-799-7233

National Fatherhood Initiative is a non-profit, non-sectarian, non-partisan organization. It conducts public awareness campaigns promoting responsible fatherhood, organizes conferences and community fatherhood forums, provides resource material to organizations seeking to establish support programs for fathers, publishes a quarterly newsletter, and disseminates informational material to men seeking to become more effective fathers. 301-948-0599; http://www.fatherhood.org

National Hispanic Prenatal Helpline 800-504-7081, 9:00 a.m.–6:00 p.m., Monday–Friday (Eastern Time)

National Immunization Information Hotline: 800-232-2522

National Institute of Child Health and Human Development Information Resource Center, 800-370-2943, 8:30 a.m.–5:00 p.m., (Eastern Time), Monday–Friday, except federal holidays

National Life Center/Pregnancy Hotline (24 hours a day), 800-848-5683

North American Council on Adoptive Children (www.nacac.org) Adoption Support, Parent Groups, Resources on Adoption.

Parental Stress National Hotline 800-367-2543

Poison Control 800-222-1222

Premature Baby Website- www.prematurity.org

Single Parent Support Groups:

• Parents Without Partners http://www.parentswithoutpartners.org

• Solo Parenting Alliance (www.solo.org)

• Sole Mothers International (home.navisoft.com/colemom/index.htm)

• Parentsplace (www.parentsplace.com)

• Single Parent Resource Center (www.singleparentresources.com)

Slowlane (www.slowlane.com) is the online resource for Stay-At-Home Dads (SAHD) and their families. Established as a reference, resource and network to assist fathers who have made (or are considering) the decision to stay home and raise their children. 850-434-2626

Social Security Administration: 800-772-1213

Teen Mother Support:

• Teen Moms: www.teenmoms.ourfamily.com Provides links to Crisis Centers and Shelters across the US, and sites that can help financially.

• Girl Mom, www.girlmom.com Support, Community and Education for young Mothers.

United States Department of Homeland Security http://www.ready.gov How to make an emergency kit, make a family plan, and be informed of potential threats to our national security. 1-800-BE-READY; www.homelandpreparedness.com

Usborne Books- Usborne books are good for all ages- from baby board books, preschool books, internet-linked books, reference books, Spanish titles, kid kits, puzzle books, history, science, encyclopedias and more! Please visit: www.littlelocalcelebrity.com and follow the link to Usborne Books! www.ubah.com/J2147

Youth Crisis Hotline 800-448-4663

Zero to Three: National Center for Infants, Toddlers and Families, 800-899-4301, 9:00 a.m.–5:00 p.m., Monday–Friday (Eastern Time) http://www.zerotothree.org/

References

[1] Field, T., Grizzle, N., Scafidi, F., Abrams, S., & Richardson, S., Kuhn, C. and Shanberg, S.(1996). Massage therapy for infants of depressed mothers. Infant Behavior and Development, 19, 109-114.

[2] Field, T. & Hernandez-Reif, M. (2001). Sleep problems in infants decrease following massage therapy. Early Child Development and Care, 168, 95-104.

[3] Field, T., Grizzle, N., Scafidi, F., Abrams, S., & Richardson, S., Kuhn, C. and Shanberg, S.(1996). Massage therapy for infants of depressed mothers. Infant Behavior and Development, 19, 109-114.

[4] Escalona, A., Field, T., Cullen, C., Hartshorn, K., & Cruz, C. (In Review). Behavior problem preschool children benefit from massage therapy. Early Child Development and Care.

[5] Cigales, M., Field, T., Lundy, B., Cuadra, A. & Hart, S. (1997). Massage enhances recovery from habituation in normal infants. Infant Behavior & Development, 20, 29-34.

[6] Laucht, Esser & Schmidt (1994)

[7] Pelaez-Nogueras, M., Gewirtz, J.L., Field, T., Cigales, M., Malphurs, J., Clasky, S., & Sanchez, A. (1996). Infant preference for touch stimulation in face-to-face interactions. Journal of Applied Developmental Psychology, 17, 199-213.

[8] Vagal refers to activity of the Vagus nerve; a cranial nerve that senses aortic blood pressure, slows heart rate, and stimulates digestive organs and taste.

[9] Field, T., Schanberg, S. M., Scafidi, F., Bauer, C. R., Vega-Lahr, N., Garcia, R., Nystrom, J., & Kuhn, C. M. (1986). Tactile/ kinesthetic stimulation effects on preterm neonates. Pediatrics, 77, 654-658.

Dieter, J., Field, T., Hernandez-Reif, M., Emory, E and Redzepi, M. (2003). Preterm infants gain more weight and sleep less following 5 days of massage therapy. Journal of Pediatric Psychology, 28, (6) 403-411.

Scafidi, F., Field, T., Schanberg, S., Bauer, C, Tucci, K., Roberts, J., Morrow, C., & Kuhn, C.M. (1990). Massage stimulates growth in preterm infants: A replication. Infant Behavior and Development, 13,167-188

[10] Field, T. (2001). Massage therapy facilitates weight gain in preterm infants. Current Directions in Psychological Science, 10, 51-54.

[11] Field, T., Hernandez-Reif, M., Seligman, S., Krasnegor, J., Sunshine, W., Rivas-Chacon, R., Schanberg, S., & Kuhn, C. (1997). Juvenile rheumatoid arthritis: benefits from massage therapy. Journal of Pediatric Psychology, 22, 607-617.

[12] Field, T., Henteleff, T., Hernandez-Reif M., Martinez, E., Mavunda, K., Kuhn C., & Schanberg S. (1998). Children with asthma have improved pulmonary functions after massage therapy. Journal of Pediatrics, 132, 854-858.

[13] Abrams, S., Field, T., & Hernandez-Reif, M. (In Review). ADHD symptoms in children are decreased following massage therapy. & Khilnani, S., Field, T., Hernandez-Reif, M., and Shanberg, S. (2004). Massage therapy improves mood and behavior of students with Attention Deficit/Hyperactivity Disorder, Adolescence, 152, 623-638.

[14] Field, T., Lasko, D, Mundy, P., Henteleff, T., Talpins, S., & Dowling, M. (1997). Autistic children's attentiveness and responsively improve after touch therapy. Journal of Autism & Developmental Disorders, 27, 333-338. & Escalona, A., Field, T., Singer-Strunck, R., Cullen, C., & Hartshorn, K. (2001). Brief report: improvements in the behavior of children with autism following massage therapy. Journal of Autism & Developmental Disorders, 31, 513-516. & Hartshorn,K., Olds, L., Field, T., Delage, J., Cullen, C. and Escalona, A. (2001) Creative movement therapy benefits children with autism. Early Child and Development and Care,166,1-5.

[15] Hernandez-Reif, M., Field, T., Largie, S., Hart, S., Redzepi, M., Nierenberg, B., & Peck, M. (2001). Children's' distress during burn treatment is reduced by massage therapy. Journal of Burn Care and Rehabilitation, 22, 191-195.

[16] Field, T., Peck, M., Krugman, S., Tucchel, T.,Shanberg, F., Kuhn, C and Burman, I. (1998). Burn injuries benefit from massage therapy. Journal of Burn Care and Rehabilitation, 19, 241-244. & Field, T., Peck, M., Hernandez-Reif, M., Krugman, S., Burman, I., & Ozment-Schenck, L. (2000). Postburn itching, pain, and psychological symptoms are reduced with massage therapy. Journal of Burn Care & Rehabilitation, 21, 189-193.

[17] Hernandez-Reif, M., Field, T., Largie, S., Diego, M., Manigat, N., Seonanes, J., Bornstein, J., & Waldman, R. (In Review). Cerebral palsy symptoms in children decreased following massage therapy. Journal of Early Intervention. & Hernandez-Reif, M., Field,T.., Largie, S., Diego, M., Manigat, N., Seonares, J., Bornstein, J and Waldman, R. (In press and 2004). Cerebral Palsy Symptoms in children decreased following a massage therapy. Early Child Development and Care

[18] Scafidi, F., Field, T., Wheeden, A., Schanberg, S., Kuhn, C., Symanski, R., Zimmerman, E., & Bandstra, E. S. (1996). Cocaine exposed preterm neonates show behavioral and hormonal differences. Pediatrics, 97, 851-855. & Jones, N.A., Field, T., Davalos, M., and Hart, S. (In press and 2004). Cocaine-exposed children show greater right frontal EEG asymmetry and non-empatheric behavior. International Journal of Neuroscience.

[19] Hernandez-Reif, M., Field, T., Krasnegor, J., & Martinez, E. (1999). Cystic fibrosis symptoms are reduced with massage therapy intervention. Journal of Pediatric Psychology, 24, 183-189.

[20] Schachner, L., Field, T., Hernandez-Reif, M., Duarte, A., & Krasnegor, J. (1998). Atopic Dermatitis Symptoms Decrease in Children Following Massage Therapy. Pediatric Dermatology, 15, 390-395.

[21] Field, T., Hernandez-Reif, M., LaGreca A., Shaw, K., Schanberg, S., & Kuhn, C. (1997). Massage therapy lowers blood glucose levels in children with Diabetes Mellitus. Diabetes Spectrum 10, 237-239.

[22] Hernandez-Reif, M., Ironson, G., Field, T., Largie, S., Deigo, M., Mora, D., & Bornstein, J. (In Review). Children with Down Syndrome improved in motor function and muscle tone following massage therapy. Journal of Early Intervention

[23] Scafidi, F. & Field, T. (1997). Massage therapy improves behavior in neonates born to HIV positive mothers. Journal of Pediatric Psychology, 21, 889-897.

[24] Field, T., Cullen, C., Diego, M., Hernandez-Reif, M., Sprinz, P., Beebe, K., Kissell, B., & Bango-Sanchez, V. (2001) Leukemia immune changes following massage therapy. Journal of Bodywork and Movement Therapy, 3, 1-5.

[25] Hernandez-Reif, M., Field, T., Field, T., & Theakston, H. (1998). Multiple Sclerosis patients benefit from massage therapy. Journal of Bodywork and Movement Therapies, 2, 168-174.

[26] Field, T., Morrow, C., Valdeon, C., Larson, S., Kuhn, C., & Schanberg, S. (1992). Massage therapy reduces anxiety in child and adolescent psychiatric patients. Journal of the American Academy of Child and Adolescent Psychiatry, 31, 125-130.

[27] Diego, M., Field, T., and Hernandez-Reif, M., Brucker, B., Hart, S., & Burman, I. (2002). Spinal cord patients benefits from massage therapy. International Journal of Neuroscience, 112,133-142.

[28] Cullen, C., Field, T., Escalona, A., & Hartshorn, K. (2000). Father-infants interactions are enhanced by massage therapy. Early Child Development and Care, 164, 41-47.

[29] Field, T., Hernandez-Reif, M., Quintino, 0., Schanberg, S. & Kuhn, C. (1998). Elder retired volunteers benefit from giving massage therapy to infants. Journal of Applied Gerontology, 17, 229-239.

[30] Field, T., Hernandez-Reif, M., Hart, S., Theakston, H., Schanberg, S., Kuhn, C., & Burman, I. (1999). Pregnant women benefit from massage therapy. Journal of Psychosomatic Obstetrics and Gynecology, 19, 31-38.

[31] Field, T., Grizzle, N., Scafidi, F., & Schanberg, S. (1996). Massage and relaxation therapies' effects on depressed adolescent mothers. Adolescence, 31, 903-911.

[32] Diego, M., Dieter, J., Field, T., Lecanuet, J., Hernandez-Reif, M., Beutler, J., Largie, S, Redzepi, M., & Salman, F. (2002). Fetal activity following vibratory stimulation of the mother's abdomen and foot and hand massage. Developmental Psychobiology, 41, 396-406.

[33] Hernandez-Reif, M., Martinez, A., Field, T., Quintino, O., Hart, S. & Burman, I. (2000). Premenstrual Syndrome symptoms are relieved by massage therapy. Journal of Psychosomatic Obstetrics and Gynecology, 21, 9-15.

[34] Field, T., T., Schanberg, S., Davalos, M. & Malphurs, J. (1996). Massage with oil has more positive effects on newborn infants. Pre and Perinatal Psychology Journal, 11, 73-78.

[35] The Oprah Winfrey Show: Keep Your Baby Safe, Airing May 31, 2002:   <http://www.oprah.com/tows/pastshows/tows_2002/tows_past_20020531_d.jhtml>

[36] The lyrics for this particular nursery rhyme include action based words where the little piggy is each one of the child's toes! The last line is used to accompany the child being tickled by the teller of the rhyme! This is a typical rhyme which will be passed down from one generation to another - it has no origins in history! The lyrics for this nursery rhyme were first published in 1728.

About the Author

Mary Grey Ady is a native Californian, transient Texan, who is currently residing in historic Mount Vernon, Virginia. She has attended Northern Virginia Community College, Hardin-Simmons University ,and George Mason University. Ms. Ady is a graduate of the nationally acclaimed Potomac Massage Training Institute in Washington D.C., and a nationally recognized Professional Member, Massage Therapist in the American Massage Therapy Association, member of the International Association of Infant Massage and a Licensed Massage Therapist, nationally and by the Board of Nursing in Virginia. Ms. Ady, is a Certified Infant Massage Instructor (CIMI), by the International Association of Infant Massage since 2000. Ms. Ady has taught infant massage classes at numerous locations in the National Capital Region, including INOVA Hospital. Ms. Ady has served as a faculty member for Heritage Institute's Associate Degree program in Massage Therapy, teaching human anatomy, physiology, kinesiology, and practical massage therapy. Readers will appreciate the thorough infant massage treatment that Ms. Ady brings to newborns and their parents, which is shown by her many years of experience and passion for this profession that has only grown exponentially since the birth of her own daughter and favorite infant massage subject, Chloe Marie, on March 15, 2005.